Flower Garden Banks
National Marine Sanctuary

CONDITION REPORT 2008

September 2008

NATIONAL MARINE
SANCTUARIES

NATIONAL MARINE
SANCTUARIES

Suggested Citation:
Office of National Marine Sanctuaries. 2008. Flower Garden Banks National Marine Sanctuary Condition Report 2008. U.S. Department of Commerce, National Oceanic and Atmospheric Administration, Office of National Marine Sanctuaries, Silver Spring, MD. 49 pp.

U.S. Department of Commerce
Carlos M. Gutierrez, Secretary

National Oceanic and Atmospheric Administration
VADM Conrad C. Lautenbacher, Jr. (USN-ret.)
Under Secretary of Commerce for Oceans and Atmosphere

National Ocean Service
John H. Dunnigan, Assistant Administrator

Office of National Marine Sanctuaries
Daniel J. Basta, Director

National Oceanic and Atmospheric Administration
Office of National Marine Sanctuaries
SSMC4, N/ORM62
1305 East-West Highway
Silver Spring, MD 20910
301-713-3125
http://sanctuaries.noaa.gov

Flower Garden Banks National Marine Sanctuary
4700 Avenue U, Building 216
Galveston, TX 77551
409-621-5151
http://flowergarden.noaa.gov

Report Preparation:

Flower Garden Banks National Marine Sanctuary, Galveston, TX:
Emma L. Hickerson, George P. Schmahl

Office of National Marine Sanctuaries, Silver Spring, MD:
Kathy Broughton, Stephen R. Gittings

Copy Editors: Matt Dozier, Kelly Drinnen, Jennifer Morgan

Graphic Designer: Matt Dozier, Matt McIntosh

Table of Contents

About this Report.. 2

Summary and Findings.. 2

National Marine Sanctuary System
and System-Wide Monitoring 3

Flower Garden Banks National Marine Sanctuary
Condition Summary Table 5

Site History and Resources
  Discovery of the Banks... 7
  Water 9
  Habitat 10
  Living Resources 12
  Maritime Archaeological Resources 13

Pressures on Sanctuary Resources
  Aquaculture and Artificial Reefs..................................... 14
  Climate Change 14
  Coral Disease 14
  Significant Regional Habitat... 15
  Harvesting... 15
  Invasive Species... 17
  Oil and Gas Infrastructure... 17
  Pollutant Discharge... 17
  Shipping and Transport.. 19
  Visitor Use 19
  Wildlife Interactions.. 19
  Hurricanes 20

State of Sanctuary Resources
  Water 21
  Habitat 24
  Living Resources 25
  Maritime Archaeological Resources 28

Response to Pressures
  Aquaculture and Artificial Reefs..................................... 29
  Climate Change 29
  Coral Disease 29
  Significant Essential Habitat... 30
  Harvesting... 30
  Invasive Species... 31
  Oil and Gas Infrastructure... 31
  Pollutant Discharge... 31
  Shipping and Transport.. 32
  Visitor Use 32
  Wildlife Interactions.. 32
  Hurricanes 32

Concluding Remarks... 33

Acknowledgements 33

Cited Resources 34
  Additional Resources... 37

Appendix: Rating Scale for
System-Wide Monitoring Questions...................................... 38

About this Report

This "condition report" provides a summary of marine resources in the National Oceanic and Atmospheric Administration's Flower Garden Banks National Marine Sanctuary, pressures on those resources, current condition and trends, and management responses to the pressures that threaten the integrity of the marine environment. Specifically, the document includes information on the status and trends of water quality, habitat, living resources and maritime archaeological resources and the human activities that affect them. It presents responses to a set of questions posed to all sanctuaries (Appendix). Resource status of the Flower Garden Banks is rated on a scale from good to poor, and the timelines used for comparison vary from topic to topic. Trends in the status of resources are also reported, and are generally based on observed changes in status over the past five years, unless otherwise specified.

To prepare this report, sanctuary staff consulted with a working group of outside experts familiar with the resources and with knowledge of previous and current scientific investigations. Evaluations of status and trends are based on interpretation of quantitative and, when necessary, non-quantitative assessments, and the observations of scientists, managers and users. The ratings reflect the collective interpretation of the status of local issues of concern among sanctuary program staff and outside experts based on their knowledge and perception of local problems. The final ratings were determined by sanctuary staff. This report has been peer reviewed and complies with the White House Office of Management and Budget's peer review standards as outlined in the Final Information Quality Bulletin for Peer Review.

This is the first attempt to describe comprehensively the status, pressures and trends of resources at the Flower Garden Banks National Marine Sanctuary. Additionally, the report helps identify gaps in current monitoring efforts, as well as causal factors that may require monitoring and potential remediation in the years to come. The data discussed will enable us to not only acknowledge prior changes in resource status, but will provide guidance for future management as we face challenges imposed by such potential threats as increasing visitor use, water quality degradation, artificial reefs and climate change.

Flower Garden Banks National Marine Sanctuary

- *56 square miles (145.38 square km)*
- *First discovered and named by fishermen*
- *Designated in 1992 as a national marine sanctuary; Stetson Bank added in 1996*
- *Complex system of outer continental shelf coral reefs, coralline algae reefs, algal nodules, and deep reefs supporting a diverse array of marine biota*
- *Unusual geological features include a brine seep that supports an associated sulfide-based community and mud volcanoes*

Summary and Findings

The East and West Flower Garden Banks have been afforded protection through the National Marine Sanctuaries Act since 1992. Prior to that, restrictions imposed by the Minerals Management Service and Environmental Protection Agency protected the banks from specific threats and activities. The sanctuary was expanded in 1996 to include Stetson Bank (Figure 1).

Regulatory decisions at the Flower Garden Banks have traditionally relied on the best information available, as well as close working relationships between scientists and resource managers. A management plan for the Flower Garden Banks was implemented with the designation of the marine sanctuary in 1992. A review of this management plan began in 2006, and is scheduled for completion by 2009. This report provides some vital information to help guide this process, and will be updated approximately every five years.

The sanctuary management plan focuses on activities that can be directly regulated or managed, though impacts taking place within the sanctuary include both human-induced and natural causes. This document outlines both natural and human activities, and evaluates impacts from both. The human activities of primary interest are research, fishing, oil and gas activities, shipping and transport, and scuba diving (Figure 2). There are also concerns that gaps in protection for other reefs and banks in the northwestern Gulf of Mexico could compromise the condition of associated assemblages throughout the region. Natural events discussed include climate change and hurricanes. Impacts from natural events can be exacerbated by human influences that reduce ecosystem resistance or resilience. Responses to these pressures by sanctuary management are also reported, and options for future management are presented.

The current conditions of the water, habitat, and living marine resources, based on research, monitoring, and anecdotal information collected over the past 40 years, are presented here. A brief history of the sanctuary is included, and pressures on sanctuary resources are discussed. The document includes a report card, indicating both the status and trends within three categories. In general, the health of most Flower Garden Banks National Marine Sanctuary resources is rated as either "good" or "good/fair." Habitat conditions were rated slightly higher than water and living resources, primarily because of recent findings

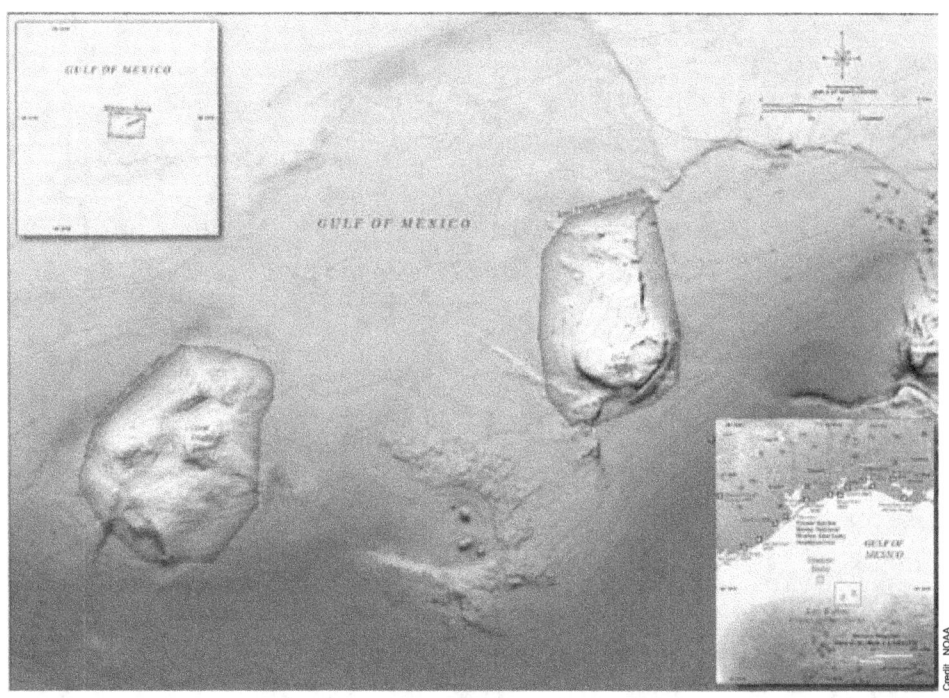

Figure 1.
Flower Garden Banks
National Marine Sanctuary
is located approximately 115
miles directly south of the
Texas-Louisiana border in
the Gulf of Mexico. Depths in
the sanctuary range from 55
- 500 feet (17-152 meters).

of high levels of ciguatoxin and mercury in fish, and concerns over apparent decreases in certain fished species and increases in the level of fishing. The Food and Drug Administration has issued a seafood advisory to seafood processors that is related directly to fish caught at and around the Flower Garden Banks National Marine Sanctuary. Also of particular concern is fishing targeting grouper, jacks and snapper, which are dominant predators in the ecosystem. One species being targeted, marbled grouper, is known to be rare throughout most of its range, but is common in certain habitats at the Flower Garden Banks. Continued targeted removal of this species could put the wider population at risk.

National Marine Sanctuary System and System-Wide Monitoring

The National Marine Sanctuary System manages marine areas in both nearshore and open ocean waters that range in size from less than one to almost 140,000 square miles. Each area has its own concerns and requirements for environmental monitoring, but ecosystem structure and function in all these areas have similarities and are influenced by common factors that interact in comparable ways. Furthermore, the human influences that affect the structure and function of these sites are similar in a number of ways. For these reasons, in 2001 the program began to implement System-Wide Monitoring (SWiM). The monitoring framework (National Marine Sanctuary Program 2004) facilitates the development of effective,

ecosystem-based monitoring programs that address management information needs using a design process that can be applied in a consistent way at multiple spatial scales and to multiple resource types. It identifies four primary components common among marine ecosystems: water, habitats, living resources and maritime archaeological resources.

By assuming that a common marine ecosystem framework can be applied to all places, the National Marine Sanctuary System developed a series of questions that are posed to every sanctuary and used as evaluation criteria to assess resource condition and trends. The questions, which are shown on the following page and explained in the Appendix, are derived from both a generalized ecosystem framework and from the National Marine Sanctuary System's mission. They are widely applicable across the system of areas managed by the sanctuary program and provide a tool with which the program can measure its progress toward maintaining and improving natural and archaeological resource quality throughout the system.

Similar reports summarizing resource status and trends will be prepared for each marine sanctuary approximately every five years and updated as new information allows. The information in this report is intended to help set the stage for the management plan review process. The report also helps sanctuary staff identify monitoring, characterization and research priorities to address gaps, day-to-day information needs and new threats.

Figure 2. A diver hovers over the coral reef at the West Flower Garden Bank. The visibility is well over 100 feet horizontally and at least 85 feet vertically, which is typical for summer conditions.

Flower Garden Banks National Marine Sanctuary
Condition Summary Table

The following table summarizes the "State of Sanctuary Resources" section of this report. The first two columns list 17 questions used to rate the condition and trends for qualities of water, habitat, living resources, and maritime archaeological resources. The "Rating" column consists of a color, indicating resource condition, and a symbol, indicating trend (see key for definitions). The "Basis for Judgment" column provides a short statement or list of criteria used to justify the rating. The "Description of Findings" column presents the statement that best characterizes resource status, and corresponds to the assigned color rating. The "Description of Findings" statements are customized for all possible ratings for each question. Please see the Appendix for further clarification of the questions and the "Description of Findings" statements.

| Status: | Good | Good/Fair | Fair | Fair/Poor | Poor | Undet. |

Trends:
Conditions appear to be improving .... ▲
Conditions do not appear to be changing .... –
Conditions appear to be declining .... ▼
Undetermined trend. .... ?
Question not applicable .... N/A

#	Questions/Resources	Rating	Basis for Judgment	Description of Findings	Sanctuary Response
WATER					
1	Are specific or multiple stressors, including changing oceanographic and atmospheric conditions, affecting water quality and how are they changing?	▼	Isolated contaminants; freshwater influxes from terrestrial sources; increased water temperature.	Selected conditions may preclude full development of living resource assemblages and habitats, but are not likely to cause substantial or persistent declines.	Existing stipulations and operating standards for oil and gas development have worked well in preventing impacts to the coral reef. Sanctuary conducts drills with MMS, training and information sharing with operators, and contingency planning with regional response authorities. Sanctuary is considering ways to limit pollutants from currently approved marine sanitation devices.
2	What is the eutrophic condition of sanctuary waters and how is it changing?	–	No evidence based on ongoing monitoring since the late 1980s.	Conditions do not appear to have the potential to negatively affect living resources or habitat quality.	
3	Do sanctuary waters pose risks to human health and how are they changing?	▼	Recent outbreaks of ciguatera traced to fish from the Flower Garden Banks; large proportion of fish tested for mercury exceeded levels for safe consumption.	Selected conditions have caused or are likely to cause severe impacts, but cases to date have not suggested a pervasive problem.	
4	What are the levels of human activities that may influence water quality and how are they changing?	–	Vessel discharges, oil and gas platform and pipeline discharges.	Some potentially harmful activities exist, but they do not appear to have had a negative effect on water quality.	
HABITAT					
5	What are the abundance and distribution of major habitat types and how are they changing?	–	Major habitat types appear to be stable, although additional monitoring in deeper communities is warranted.	Habitats are in pristine or near-pristine condition and are unlikely to preclude full community development.	Recent emphasis on high-resolution mapping and characterization of habitats within and adjacent to the three sanctuary units, as well as on other banks of the northwestern Gulf of Mexico. IMO designation of the Flower Garden Banks as a "No Anchor" area should reduce risk of anchoring by foreign-flagged vessels. Trained naturalists on board dive charters conduct education about sanctuary resources in order to reduce impacts and enrich visitor experience.
6	What is the condition of biologically structured habitats and how is it changing?	–	Damage by anchoring; lost or discarded fishing gear and cables, mostly in deep habitats; destabilization by fishing gear and/or anchors at Stetson Bank.	Selected habitat loss or alteration has taken place, precluding full development of living resources, but it is unlikely to cause substantial or persistent degradation in living resources or water quality.	
7	What are the contaminant concentrations in sanctuary habitats and how are they changing?	?	Limited investigations suggest low levels of contaminants.	Contaminants do not appear to have the potential to negatively affect living resources or water quality.	
8	What are the levels of human activities that may influence habitat quality and how are they changing?	–	Limited number of dive charters, some fishing gear impacts, some illegal fishing.	Some potentially harmful activities exist, but they do not appear to have had a negative effect on habitat quality.	

Table is continued on the following page.

Flower Garden Banks National Marine Sanctuary Condition Summary Table (Continued)

#	Questions/Resources	Rating	Basis for Judgment	Description of Findings	Sanctuary Response
LIVING RESOURCES					
9	What is the status of biodiversity and how is it changing?	–	Long-term monitoring of coral reef communities and other information collected since the 1970s.	Biodiversity appears to reflect pristine or near-pristine conditions and promotes ecosystem integrity (full community development and function).	Monitoring program is adequate for the most part for the coral reef, but may need enhancements to deal with emerging threats (e.g., impacts of offshore aquaculture, acidification and other effects of climate change). There is a need to expand the monitoring effort into the deepwater habitats below the coral reef zone. Current focus is on coral disease and bleaching frequency and impacts, and removal of non-indigenous species when they are encountered. Recent designation of sanctuary areas as essential fish habitat, combined with outreach and education efforts, increase protection options and awareness of resource threats. Enforcement capability will be enhanced with the addition of a sanctuary vessel in 2008.
10	What is the status of environmentally sustainable fishing and how is it changing?	?	Unpublished observations suggest a decline in certain species of fish, e.g., grouper and jacks.	Extraction may inhibit full community development and function and may cause measurable but not severe degradation of ecosystem integrity.	
11	What is the status of non-indigenous species and how is it changing?	–	Recent invasive species have been discovered, but abundances are low and there is no evidence that they have become established in natural areas.	Non-indigenous species exist, precluding full community development and function, but are unlikely to cause substantial or persistent degradation of ecosystem integrity.	
12	What is the status of key species and how is it changing?	?	Coral, mantas and sea turtles appear to be stable. Hammerhead, grouper, snapper, and jacks may be declining. *Diadema* sea urchin populations remain depressed since the 1983-84 die-off.	Selected key or keystone species are at reduced levels, perhaps precluding full community development and function, but substantial or persistent declines are not expected.	
13	What is the condition or health of key species and how is it changing?	▼	Observations of coral disease for four straight years, though no apparent population impact to date; loss of some *Millepora alcicornis* due to bleaching.	The condition of selected key resources is not optimal, perhaps precluding full ecological function, but substantial or persistent declines are not expected.	
14	What are the levels of human activities that may influence living resource quality and how are they changing?	?	Stable levels of recreational diving, apparent increase and effectiveness of private and commercial fishing; no monitoring of use levels is in place.	Selected activities have resulted in measurable living resource impacts, but evidence suggests effects are localized, not widespread.	
MARITIME ARCHAEOLOGICAL RESOURCES					
15	What is the integrity of known maritime archaeological resources and how is it changing?	N/A	No documented underwater archeological sites.	N/A	N/A
16	Do known maritime archaeological resources pose an environmental hazard and how is this threat changing?	N/A	No documented underwater archeological sites.	N/A	
17	What are the levels of human activities that may influence maritime archaeological resource quality and how are they changing?	N/A	No documented underwater archeological sites.	N/A	

Site History and Resources

Overview

Located in the northwestern Gulf of Mexico, Flower Garden Banks National Marine Sanctuary includes three separate areas, known as East Flower Garden, West Flower Garden and Stetson Banks. The banks range in depth from 55 to nearly 500 feet (16 to 150 meters), perched atop underwater hills formed by rising domes of ancient salt, and support several distinct habitats, including the northernmost coral reefs in the continental United States. These and other similar formations throughout the northwestern Gulf of Mexico provide the foundation for essential habitat for a variety of tropical and temperate species.

The combination of location and geology makes the Flower Garden Banks extremely productive and diverse, and presents a unique set of challenges for managing and protecting its natural wonders.

Discovery of the Banks

The Flower Garden Banks have a rich but comparatively short history of exploration and discovery. Although snapper fishermen in the early 1900s nicknamed the area the Texas Flower Gardens because of the brightly colored "rocks" (corals) that were visible through the clear water, the first official documentation of the banks did not occur until the 1930s. For the next 30 years, the banks were occasionally included as part of investigations of larger portions of the Gulf of Mexico. Despite these investigations and rumors of coral reefs from the fishing community, many scientists believed that any coral reefs located here must be dead, primarily because of the depth and water temperatures.

Then, in the 1960s, expeditions conducted by the Houston Museum of Natural Science, the U.S. Navy and volunteer divers settled the debate. Divers visited the reefs and brought back specimens and reports of living, healthy coral reefs that were stunning in their beauty.

Exploration of the area soon began in earnest, as the banks became a popular spot for both researchers and recreational divers. They soon discovered a wealth of coral reef species, some of which are only rarely seen elsewhere (Figures 3 and 4).

As new technology allowed oil and gas production to move offshore into deeper water in the 1970s, concerns about detrimental impacts to the reefs increased. The Minerals Management Service established "No Activity Zones" around most of the banks in the northern Gulf of Mexico. While these measures controlled impacts from oil- and gas-related activities, they did not cover activities such as diving, anchoring, fishing and shipping. The recreational dive community took action to address anchoring issues and formed the Gulf Reef Environmental Action Team (GREAT). This group raised funds and recruited volunteers to install mooring buoys. These and other divers also offered their services to researchers involved in charac-

Figure 3. The marbled grouper (*Dermatolepis inermis*) is considered a rare grouper throughout its range. The IUCN Red List Categories and Criteria is a system for classifying species at high risk of global extinction. Based on the information provided by the sanctuary, the marbled grouper was upgraded from Least Concern to Near Threatened by the IUCN.

Figure 4. The coral reef community and its associates include algae, sponges, worms, crabs, lobsters, shellfish, sea urchins, fish, sharks, rays, sea turtles, and marine mammals. Large schools of jacks and the presence of large grouper make this reef even more enjoyable for divers.

terizing and monitoring the banks. Nevertheless, continued anchoring by large ships and impacts from certain types of fishing made it apparent that additional formal protection was needed. It would take the combined efforts of recreational divers, researchers, federal agencies and advocates in congress to get the Flower Garden Banks designated as a national marine sanctuary in 1992.

A strong tradition of discovery and community involvement continues today. The sanctuary science team, in concert with a wide array of partners, continues to explore, study, and monitor the sanctuary ecosystems, as well as those around it that are most likely to influence the sanctuary's continued health.

East and West Flower Garden Banks

The Flower Garden Banks are unique among ecosystems in the Gulf of Mexico. They contain the northernmost coral reefs in the continental United States. The nearest neighboring tropical coral reefs are 400 miles (643 km) away in the Bay of Campeche, off the Yucatan peninsula of Mexico, while the closest U.S. coral reefs are located 750 miles (1,207 km) southeast, in the Florida Keys.

East Flower Garden Bank is a pear-shaped dome, 5.4 by 3.2 miles (8.7 by 5.1 km) in size, capped by 354 acres (1.43 square km) of coral reef that rise to within 55 feet (17 meters) of the surface. West Flower Garden Bank is an oblong-shaped dome, 6.8 by 5 miles (11 by 8 km) that includes 102 acres (0.42 square km) of coral reef area starting 59 feet (18 meters) below the surface.

Brain and star corals dominate the coral caps of the Flower Garden Banks, with a few coral heads exceeding 20 feet (6 meters) in diameter. There are at least 21 species of coral on the coral cap, covering over 50% of the bottom to depths of 100 feet (30 meters) (Bright et al. 1984, Continental Shelf Assoc., Inc. 1996, Gittings 1998, Dokken et al. 1999, Dokken et al. 2003, Schmahl 2002, Pattengill-Semmens and Gittings 2003, Schmahl and Hickerson 2004, Aronson et al. 2005, Hickerson and Schmahl 2005), and exceeding 70% coral cover in places to at least 130 feet (40 meters) (Precht et al. 2005). Interestingly, the coral caps do not contain some species commonly found elsewhere in the Caribbean, such as many of the branching corals, sea whips or sea fans. In fact, despite the high cover, only about a third of Caribbean hard coral species are found in the Flower Garden Banks National Marine Sanctuary.

A recent observation of note is the discovery of two live *Acropora palmata* colonies, one each on the East and West Flower Garden Banks. These discoveries are some of the deepest records of these species (Zimmer et al. 2006).

Less well-known is the deepwater habitat of the Flower Garden Banks that makes up over 98% of the area within the sanctuary boundaries. Habitats below recreational scuba limits include algal-sponge zones, "honeycomb" reefs (highly eroded outcroppings),

mud flats, mounds, mud volcanoes and at least one brine seep system. Different assemblages of sea life reside in these deeper habitats, including extensive beds of coralline algae pavements and algal nodules, colorful sea fans, sea whips and black corals, deep reef fish, batfish, sea robins, basket stars and feather stars.

Stetson Bank

Stetson Bank is located 70 miles (113 km) south of Galveston, Texas, and 30 miles (48 km) to the northwest of West Flower Garden Bank. Depths at Stetson Bank range from about 55 feet (17 meters) to 194 feet (59 meters). Environmental conditions at Stetson Bank, which include more extreme fluctuations in temperature and turbidity than at the Flower Garden Banks, do not support the growth of reef forming corals like those found at East and West Flower Garden Banks. Divers have described Stetson as having a "moonscape" appearance, with distinct pinnacles that push out of the seafloor for 1,500 feet (457 meters) along the northwest face of the bank. An area referred to as the "flats" stretches out behind the pinnacles region, and is dotted with low relief outcroppings.

The pinnacles of Stetson Bank are dominated by fire coral (Figure 5) and sponges, with cover exceeding 30% (Bernhardt 2000). There are at least nine coral species at Stetson Bank, but with the exception of fire coral and a large area of *Madracis decactis*, most colonies are small and sparsely distributed. Algae, sponges and rubble dominate the flats.

A ring of claystone outcroppings forming a halo around the main feature of Stetson Bank (Gardner et al. 1998) was identified through surveys after the designation of the sanctuary boundaries. Sponges, gorgonians and black corals dominate this impressive ring of outcroppings between 165 and 196 feet (50 - 60 meters). Deep reef fish and invertebrates are prominent inhabitants of the "Stetson Ring." Much of the feature is out-

Figure 5. A pair of French angelfish (*Pomacanthus paru*) swims over a typical fire coral (*Millepora alcicornis*) dominated pinnacle at Stetson Bank.

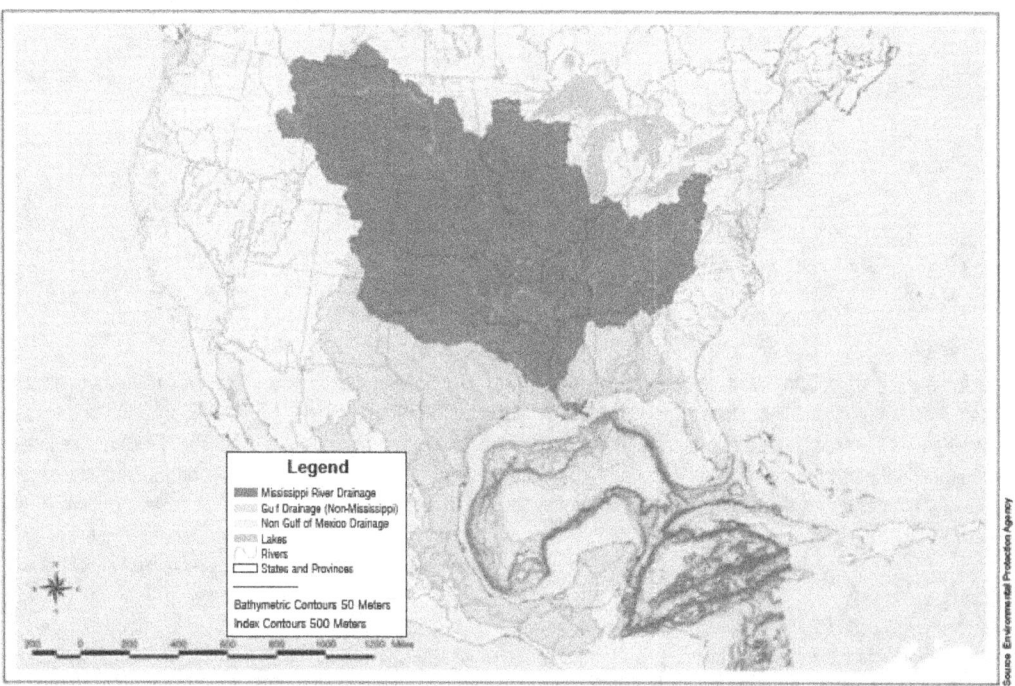

Figure 6. Gulf of Mexico watershed.

side of the current sanctuary boundaries, an issue that has been identified as a priority to rectify through the management plan review.

Water

East and West Flower Garden Banks and Stetson Bank are three among dozens of banks scattered along the continental shelf throughout the northwestern Gulf of Mexico. All of these banks are part of a regional ecosystem heavily influenced by current patterns within the Gulf. Inflows from the large Mississippi and Atchafalaya watersheds also play a significant role in the health of this region.

Currents

From the south, the Gulf of Mexico is fed by warm water from the Caribbean, which enters the Gulf between Mexico's Yucatan Peninsula and Cuba. Called the Yucatan Current, this water flows northward before turning east then south along Florida's west coast, forming the Gulf Loop Current and exiting through the Straits of Florida.

The Yucatan Current is variable, sometimes barely entering the Gulf before turning east, and at other times traveling almost to Louisiana's coast before swinging toward Florida. Frequently, meanders of the Gulf Loop Current (which is what the Yucatan Current is called

after it enters the Gulf) break away from the main current and form circular eddies that move westward, generally slightly to the south of the Flower Garden, Stetson and other banks to the west. These currents help distribute animal larvae, plant spores and other imports from the south, which accounts in part for the many Caribbean species found in the northern Gulf of Mexico (Lugo-Fernandez et al. 2001, Gold et al. 2004, Sammarco et al. 2004). As it continues, the loop current also carries with it "passengers" from the northern Gulf to destinations along its route to the Atlantic.

Meanwhile, shallow tropical waters of the southern Gulf of Mexico move northward along the Mexican coast into Texas before turning east. These wind-driven currents also cross over the Flower Garden, Stetson and other banks and add to the tropical influence in the region.

Watershed

Multiple rivers emptying into the Gulf of Mexico drain the interior of North America (as much as two-thirds of the United States) (Figure 6). These rivers bring with them all of the runoff accumulated from cities, suburbs, agricultural areas and wild lands along their routes. Before reaching the Gulf, this water source is partially depleted by

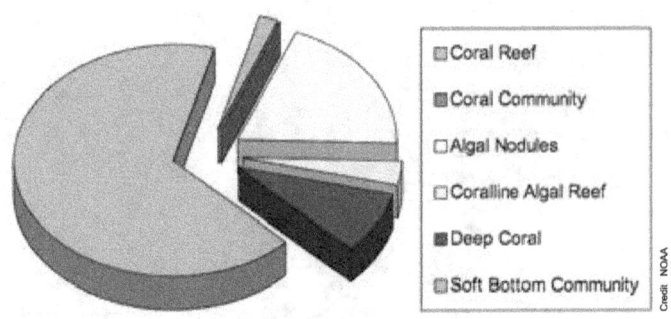

Figure 7. The primary biological habitats within the Flower Garden Banks National Marine Sanctuary.

extractions for municipal, industrial and agricultural consumption, thus reducing freshwater inflows that sustain the estuaries. When healthy, the estuaries filter sediments and pollutants from the water, export organic material for the nearshore food chain, and provide nursery areas for many species, some of which later move offshore to the system of banks along the continental shelf.

Connectivity

Studies of physical oceanography have demonstrated that water flow connects the dozens of banks along the continental shelf of the northwestern Gulf of Mexico. More specifically, rates and patterns of current flow in the region make it likely that the larvae and spores of many animals and plants disperse from bank to bank and perhaps to or from features elsewhere in the Gulf of Mexico (Lugo-Fernandez 1998). Observations show that reef corals, probably originating at the Flower Garden Banks, attach and grow on petroleum platforms in the northwestern Gulf (Bright et al. 1991). Biogeographic investigations showing high similarity in habitats at similar depths in the region further support the likelihood of ecological connections between features (Rezak et al. 1985, Gittings et al. 1992a).

Recent explorations, however, indicate that there may be an even greater physical connection than previously known. Technological advances have allowed higher resolution mapping, which has revealed systems of low-relief geological features (such as rock outcroppings) between some banks. Some have been explored in the last few years, and it appears that they may serve as direct connections between the banks. Transitory species such as jacks have been observed feeding on fish along these deep outcrops, presumably as they move between the larger features of the region. As we build upon the knowledge established by the discoveries to date, we may discover that these interactions play a crucial role in maintaining the health of the sanctuary's living marine resources.

Added to this are the thousands of oil and gas production platforms in the northwestern Gulf that serve as artificial reefs by providing hard surfaces to which larvae and spores may attach. Platforms also provide substrate for range expansions of tropical species, such as the sergeant major (*Abudefduf saxatilis*) and tessellated blenny (*Hypsoblennius invemar*) (Pattengill 1998), as well as invasive species, such as the orange cup coral (*Tubastraea coccinea*) (Fenner and Banks 2004) and certain barnacles (Gittings 1985). Scientists are still assessing the extent to which this system of platforms affects the overall biological diversity and productivity of the Gulf.

Habitat

The primary biological habitats within the sanctuary boundaries are as follows (Figure 7):

■ Coral Reef: 1.03 square miles (2.68 sq. km), representing 1.84% of the area within the sanctuary. Over 50% coral coverage, representing a remarkably healthy reef system.

■ Coral Community (i.e., non-reef-building): 0.019 square miles (0.05 sq. km), representing 0.03% of the area within the sanctuary.

■ Coralline Algae Zone:
  • Algal nodules: 11 square miles (28.27 sq. km), representing 19.45% of the area within the sanctuary.
  • Coralline Algal reef: 1.9 square miles (4.98 sq. km), representing 3.43% of the area within the sanctuary.

■ Deep Coral: 4.78 square miles (12.37 sq. km) representing 8.51% of the area within the sanctuary.

■ Soft Bottom Community: 37.4 square miles (96.95 sq. km) representing 66.69% of the area within the sanctuary.

Coral Reef Zone

The coral reef zone is the shallowest zone at the Flower Garden Banks, occurring at depths of between approximately 55 and 145 feet (17 to 44 meters). It is dominated by large, closely spaced star and brain coral heads, many up to 10 or more feet (greater than 3 meters) in diameter and height. Reef topography is relatively rough, with many vertical and inclined surfaces and crevices. Between groups of coral heads, there are numerous sand patches and channels. This is the part of the sanctuary most familiar to visitors.

This zone is characterized by a high diversity coral assemblage dominated by *Montastraea* spp., *Diploria strigosa*, *Colpophyllia natans* and *Porites astreoides*. Coralline algae, and filamentous and leafy algae also occur on reef substrates, but are not dominant members of the benthic assemblage. *Madracis mirabilis* forms large monotypic stands in deeper portions of the coral reef community. Sponges and *Agaricia* spp. are common in crevices and cavities of the reef.

Coral Community Zone

The coral community zone is comprised of areas that, while not considered to be "true" coral reefs, do contain hermatypic (reef-building) coral species at low densities, or are characterized by other coral reef associated organisms, such as the hydrozoan *Millepora* spp. (fire coral), sponges and macroalgae. Coral communities are found in depth ranges similar to those that contain coral reefs (55 to 165 feet/17 to 50 meters), where other environmental factors have not allowed full development of coral reefs. The "coral community" includes the "*Millepora*-sponge" zone described by Rezak et al. (1985), and also includes some other coral associated assemblages. Stetson Bank is dominated by this community type between 55 and 139 feet (17 to 42 meters).

The coral community at the Flower Garden Banks (formerly known as the low-diversity coral reef) is characterized by the blushing star coral, (*Stephanocoenia intersepta*), the great star coral, (*Montastraea cavernosa*), and the large grooved brain coral, (*Colpophyllia natans*), and occurs between depths of 132 and 182 feet (40 to 55 meters). The lettuce corals (*Agaricia* spp.) and brain coral (*Diploria strigosa*) are also an important part of the community. Crustose coralline algae are the dominant encrusting form on dead coral rock, along with leafy algae and numerous sponges. The dominance of hard corals declines with depth, and few coral colonies occur between 148 to165 feet (45 to 50 meters) at East and West Flower Garden Banks. Coral communities at Stetson Bank are dominated by the *Millepora*-sponge assemblage, along with areas of *Madracis decactis* and individual colonies of *Diploria strigosa* and several other coral species.

Coralline Algae Zone

Found in depths between 148 and 297 feet (45 to 90 meters), the coralline algae zone is made up of algal nodule fields, pavements and coralline algal reefs. Coralline algae occurs within the photic zone above approximately 280 feet (85 meters), as coralline algae is a photosynthetic organism (i.e., requires light to survive). This zone is biologically rich in sponges, algae, gorgonians, and black coral and harbors healthy populations of deep reef fish including rough tongue bass (*Pronotogrammus martinicensis*), scamp (*Mycteroperca phenax*), and marbled grouper (*Dermatolepis inermis*).

The coralline algae zone at the Flower Garden Banks (including the area formerly known as the "algal sponge zone") is dominated by crustose coralline algae that form large beds of algal nodules (also called "rhodoliths"), or massive reef structures composed of large plates and ridges. A variety of sponge species are abundant in this zone, along with numerous antipatharians (black corals) and octocorals (sea whips). Few reef building corals occur at these depths, and are primarily limited to small isolated colonies.

Deep Coral Zone

Found in depths typically below 295 feet (90 meters), the deep coral zone is dominated by eroded reef outcroppings, azooxanthellate (non-reef building) solitary hard corals, antipatharian and gorgonian corals, deep reef fish, sponges, bryozoans, and crinoids (feather stars).

The deep coral community at the Flower Garden Banks (formerly known as the "drowned reef" zone) occurs below water depths that support active photosynthesis. Rock surfaces are often highly eroded, and lack coralline algal growth. The deep coral zone is sometimes characterized by turbid water conditions, and reef outcrops may often be covered with a thin layer of silt (particularly at Stetson Bank).

Soft Bottom Community Zone

Large expanses of mud, sand, and silt substrates, which typify the soft bottom community zone, are found in the deepest parts of the banks and surrounding the banks. Features of the soft bottom community include pits, burrows, *Cirrhipathes* (*Stichopathes*) fields, stalked anemones, and echinoderms. Squat lobster (*Munida* sp.) are often observed in this zone.

Deeper areas of the sanctuary are characterized by a soft, level bottom composed of both terrigenous sediments originating from coastal rivers and carbonate sediments resulting from calcareous planktonic remains and erosion of rocky outcrops and coral reef communities. Soft bottom communities are often characterized by sand waves, burrows and mounds. Transitional zones between soft bottom communities and hard bottom features are characterized by exposed rubble, isolated patch reefs or exposed hard bottom. Areas with buried or exposed carbonate rubble are often colonized by antipatharians, octocorals, or solitary hard corals. Soft bottom communities serve as important feeding areas for reef and reef-associated fishes (Rexing 2006).

Figure 8. Terminal male phase of the Mardi Gras wrasse (*Halichoeres burekae*). Avid fish counters put this species of fish at the top of their list to watch for during their dives at all three banks of the sanctuary.

Figure 9. Golden smooth trunkfish (*Lactophrys triqueter*).

Figure 10. Loggerhead sea turtle (*Caretta caretta*) feeds on sponge (*Chondrilla* sp.) at Stetson Bank.

Living Resources
Fish

The benthic habitat of Flower Garden Banks National Marine Sanctuary provides critical protection, food, and shelter for the associated fish community. At least 280 species of fish have been documented within the sanctuary, including colorful reef inhabitants such as parrotfish, wrasse, angelfish, boxfish, smooth trunkfish and squirrelfish (Bright and Pequegnat 1974, Pattengill 1998). Large schools of barracuda (*Sphyraena barracuda*) and pelagic jacks (*Caranx* spp.) greet divers as they enter the waters of the sanctuary in the summer. Winter brings enormous schools of mackerel (*Scomberomorus* sp.). The conspicuous deeper water fish in the sanctuary include rough tongue bass, threadnose bass, vermillion snapper, red snapper, scamp, and marbled grouper. Commercially targeted species include snapper, grouper, jacks, and mackerel.

In June 1997, the "Mardi Gras wrasse" (*Halichoeres burekae*) was first observed by divers from the Reef Environmental Education Foundation (REEF) at East Flower Garden Bank, and subsequently in schools at Stetson Bank (Weaver and Rocha 2007) (Figure 8). This wrasse turned out to be not only new to the Flower Garden Banks National Marine Sanctuary, but also new to science. The wrasse has also been reported from the reefs of Vera Cruz, Mexico, in the southern Gulf of Mexico.

Smooth trunkfish (*Lactophrys triqueter*) are common throughout the Caribbean, but the golden morph of the species is very rare (Pattengill-Semmens 1999) (Figure 9). It was first described at the Flower Garden Banks, and has since been rumored to occur in just one other place in the Caribbean.

Sea Turtles

Loggerhead and hawksbill sea turtles reside at all three banks of the sanctuary throughout the year. Loggerheads (*Caretta caretta*) are most often seen at night or in the late afternoon resting underneath ledges or coral heads (Figure 10). In the early morning they often leave the reef to feed in deeper areas of the sanctuary (Hickerson 2000). They can also be seen on the surface catching a breath. Sea turtles surface about once an hour for a couple of minutes, and then submerge to sleep or forage.

The most frequently observed loggerheads are juveniles approaching maturity, perhaps suggesting that the sanctuary reefs serve as a temporary residence for these animals while they prepare to move on to adult feeding areas. Adult female loggerheads have also been sighted on several occasions. Recent satellite and radio tracking studies have shown that while resident at the banks, loggerhead sea turtles have home ranges that are quite specific, but not entirely within sanctuary boundaries (Hickerson 2000).

Because hawksbill sea turtles (*Eretmochelys imbricata*) are primarily sponge-eaters, Stetson Bank offers an abundant food source

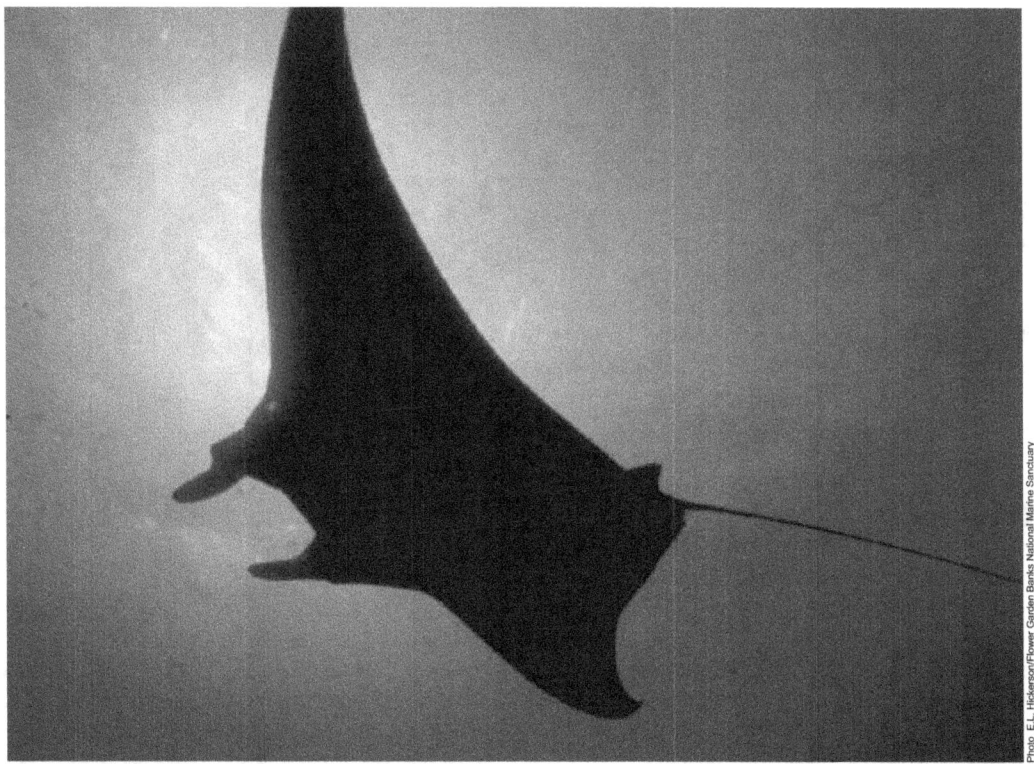

Photo: E.L. Hickerson/Flower Garden Banks National Marine Sanctuary

Figure 11. Manta rays (*Manta birostris*) are encountered by divers year-round at the sanctuary.

and is likely an excellent habitat for these turtles. A young hawksbill sea turtle has been a resident of Stetson Bank since 1999. A small number of transient hawksbills have also been reported at both the Flower Garden Banks and Stetson Bank (Hickerson 2000).

Sharks & Rays

Approximately 20 species of sharks and rays have been documented at the Flower Garden and Stetson Banks, some seasonal, others year-round (Childs 2001). During the winter months, schooling scalloped hammerhead sharks (*Sphyrna lewini*) and spotted eagle rays (*Aetobatus narinari*) are visitors to all three banks. The reason for the seasonality of their visits is unclear, but the occurrence is quite predictable. Other winter visitors include occasional sandbar (*Carcharhinus plumbeus*) and tiger sharks (*Galeocerdo cuvier*), as well as spinner sharks (*Carcharhinus brevipinna*), which are often seen leaping out of the water. Summer months usually bring whale sharks (*Rhincodon typus*) to the area. These filter-feeding creatures can reach over 30 feet (9 meters) in length. Nurse sharks are sometimes seen resting under ledges or in crevices in the coral, while large schools of silky sharks (*Carcharhinus falciformis*) are known to aggregate around oil and gas platforms in the vicinity of the sanctuary during the winter months. Silky sharks have recently been observed in large schools, exhibiting mating behavior at Stetson Bank.

Manta (*Manta birostris*) and the very similar-looking mobula rays (*Mobula* spp.) are regular visitors to the sanctuary (Figure 11). At least 58 different individuals have been documented and identified by distinctive markings on their undersides. Recent acoustic tracking of the manta rays has revealed that the mantas are moving between at least the three banks of the sanctuary — an animal that was tagged on Stetson Bank appeared on the East Bank, and then the West Bank, 30 to 40 miles (48 to 64 km) away from Stetson Bank (R. Graham, pers. comm.). While it is known that these species move between banks, it is unknown to what extent these and other migratory animals utilize other banks in the region.

Maritime Archaeological Resources

To date, imagery and documentation of Flower Garden Banks National Marine Sanctuary reveals no evidence of submerged archaeological artifacts.

Pressures on Sanctuary Resources

Numerous human activities and natural events and processes affect the condition of natural resources in marine sanctuaries. This section describes the nature and extent of the most prominent pressures on the Flower Garden Banks National Marine Sanctuary.

Aquaculture and Artificial Reefs

Recently, there have been proposals to utilize offshore oil and gas platforms for aquaculture (fish farming); however, none have yet been undertaken. There is also an active artificial reef program in Texas and Louisiana. Some artificial reefs have already been located in close proximity (within seven miles) of the sanctuary. It is unknown to what extent either of these activities may affect ecosystem function, including processes such as invasive species dispersal, disease frequency in fish and invertebrates, parasite loads, competition, and recruitment. Experiences elsewhere suggest they may be causes for concern. There are currently 15 active oil and gas platforms within the Minerals Management Service four-mile zone encompassing the sanctuary. These platforms provide artificial substrate for organisms including sponges, bryozoans, barnacles, hydroids, corals, and associated fish communities. The oil and gas platforms as well as mooring buoys have provided shallow water habitat for early life history stages of fishes, e.g. sergeant majors (*Abudefduf saxatilis*), and have allowed for some species to increase their ranges into areas where they did not previously exist (e.g., yellowtail snapper, *Ocyurus chrysurus*) — a form of range extension referred to as "island hopping" (Pattengill 1998). The artificial reef structure has also been documented as the probable vector source for the spread of an invasive coral species, the orange cup coral (*Tubastraea coccinea*) (Fenner 2004). An active gas platform, High Island A389A (HIA389A), is located one mile from the reef cap of East Flower Garden Bank, and has extensive colonies of orange cup coral. In 2002 the species was first documented on the natural reef habitat of East Flower Garden Bank. To date, no orange cup coral has been reported from West Flower Garden Bank.

Villareal et al. (2007) reported that the increased substrate availability provided by the oil and gas industry in the Gulf of Mexico has contributed to the increased levels of ciguatoxins regionally, leading to increased incidents of ciguatera poisoning.

Climate Change

Human-induced increases in greenhouse gas emissions are contributing to global-scale warming and are associated with acidification of the world's oceans (Orr et al. 2005). For corals, warming events have the potential to cause or exacerbate harmful events, such as outbreaks of disease and coral bleaching, and may reduce growth or impair sexual reproduction.

Corals typically respond to elevated seawater temperatures and other stressors by "bleaching," undergoing physiological changes that result in them expelling their algal symbionts (Figure 12). Historically, the corals within the Flower Garden Banks National Marine Sanctu-

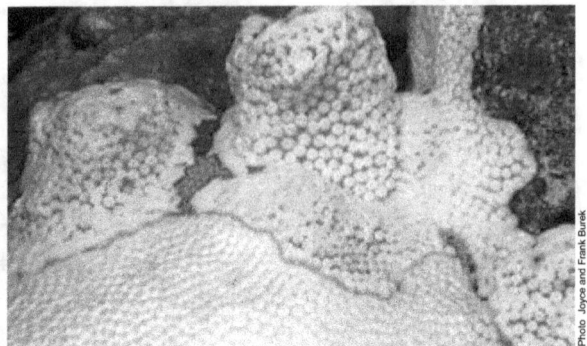

Figure 12. Bleached great star coral, *Montastraea cavernosa*, photographed during the 2005 bleaching event at the sanctuary.

ary have proven to be resilient following bleaching events. However, in 2005 the worst bleaching event on record occurred, and approximately 45 percent of the coral colonies at the Flower Garden Banks National Marine Sanctuary were affected. Mortality was not high overall, but concerns exist over this apparently increasing threat. The coral bleaching during this event diminished below a depth of approximately 95 feet (29 meters), indicating that deeper regions of the reef are less susceptible to factors that cause coral bleaching.

Coral Disease

Coral reefs throughout the world have been impacted by a variety of diseases, some of which have decimated coral populations in

Figure 13. Example of the coral disease affecting corals in the sanctuary during the winters of 2005-07. This image of a star coral, (*Montastraea franksi),* illustrates the typical visual indicators of the coral disease.

certain areas. In general, most aspects of these diseases are poorly known. Until recently, very little coral disease has been documented at the Flower Garden Banks National Marine Sanctuary, probably due to many factors, including distance from shore and excellent water quality. However, within the last several years, a number of incidences of coral disease at the Flower Garden Banks have been documented (Figure 13). Maintaining water quality at the Flower Garden Banks is critical, as there is evidence from other locations that coral disease severity can increase when reef waters contain elevated nutrient levels. This is probably because the nutrients promote pathogen growth, enhancing their fitness and thus virulence (Bruno 2003).

Significant Regional Habitat

Recent high-resolution multi-beam bathymetric surveys have revealed hard bottom features outside the current sanctuary boundaries that are structurally connected to the geological and biological resources within the sanctuary. An example of the Stetson Bank "ring" has been previously discussed. The Stetson Bank boundaries were created prior to the mapping that revealed the ring around Stetson Bank. The ring is clearly part of the structure of Stetson Bank, and remotely operated vehicle (ROV) surveys have documented the outcroppings and associated biological communities making up the feature. The Sanctuary Advisory Council has recommended adjusting the Stetson Bank boundaries to encompass this ring feature. This will also align sanctuary regulations and boundaries with the Habitat Area of Particular Concern boundaries encompassing Stetson Bank.

Surveys have also revealed an extensive area of hundreds of patch reefs, forming a horseshoe-shaped feature, located between East and West Flower Garden Banks. Mud volcanoes also were revealed through bathymetric surveys and verified through ROV surveys. These features, many of which contain hard substrates, harbor rich assemblages of black corals, octocorals, and deep reef fish, and offer opportunities for movement between the banks by pelagic animals as intermediate locations for feeding and shelter (Hickerson 2000). Some also have been found to contain habitats for juvenile groupers found as adults on the Flower Garden Banks. These "habitat highways" may prove to be critical to the success of the reefs and banks of the northwestern Gulf of Mexico and should be considered for further protection.

Harvesting
Fishing

The impacts of fishing and associated fishing activities on the sanctuary have not been precisely documented at the Flower Garden Banks. Conventional hook and line fishing is allowed in the sanctuary. However, illegal fishing by both commercial longliners

and recreational spearfishermen has been documented. Lost or tangled bottom fishing gear has been found on numerous occasions, as well as discarded spear heads, and even a lost speargun. Targeted fishing efforts, which are allowed under current regulations, could have a detrimental impact on snapper, grouper, mackerel and jack populations, especially if directed at spawning aggregations. A possible bycatch effect could explain the apparent reduction in hammerhead shark numbers. Fishermen have reported that while they were fishing for snapper and grouper during the winter, all they could catch were hammerheads. It is unknown what the fates of these animals were after release. Observations by long-time divers within the sanctuary suggest that there has been a substantial decline in certain species of fish that are commonly targeted by fishers in recent years, including red snapper (*Lutjanus campechanus*), large groupers (*Mycteroperca* sp.) and amberjacks (*Seriola dumerili*). Technological advances in vessel design and equipment (Global Positioning Systems, advanced fish finders, braided fishing line, etc.) have made it easier to find and catch fish in areas that were previously difficult to access.

Recreational fishing can have a major impact on fish populations (Figure 14). In the Gulf of Mexico, recreational fishers account for up to 64 percent of the total catch of fish species of concern (Coleman et al. 2004). The red snapper stock is "overfished" and has been undergoing overfishing in the Gulf of Mexico since the late 1980s. Of the 15 grouper species that are fished regularly in the Gulf of Mexico, the health of only four of these populations has been assessed: red (*Epinephelus morio*), gag (*Mycteroperca microlepis*), goliath (*Epinephelus itajara*) and yellowedge (*Epinephelus flavolimbatus*). Of these, the gag grouper is considered overfished, the goliath grouper was previously considered overfished (but is now recovering due to a total prohibition of take of this species), and the yellowedge grouper

Figure 14. Official IFGA world record and Texas state record marbled grouper (*Dermatolepis inermis*), caught July 16, 2006, at the Flower Garden Banks by Scott Anderson (pictured).

Figure 15. Carcharinid shark discarded on Stetson Bank.

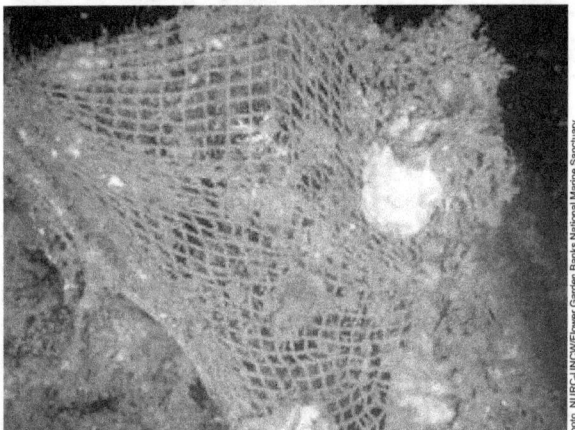

Figure 16. Discarded shrimping net within the Flower Garden Banks National Marine Sanctuary.

population status is "unknown." Red grouper are under a rebuilding plan as a result of being declared overfished in 1997. In 2002, a stock assessment concluded that red grouper were still undergoing overfishing, though no longer in an overfished condition. Red grouper does not normally occur in the vicinity of the Flower Garden Banks. Population assessments of the other species of grouper in the Gulf of Mexico have not been conducted. Greater amberjack (*Seriola dumerili*) have been under a rebuilding plan in the Gulf of Mexico since 2003. A new stock assessment in 2006 concluded the stock is not recovering as projected; it is overfished and is still undergoing overfishing. Given the state of overfishing in the Gulf of Mexico, it is reasonable to expect that similar fishing impacts are occurring at the Flower Garden Banks. Marbled grouper (*Dermatolepis inermis*), a species of particular concern, is seen frequently by divers

at the Flower Garden Banks, and has been documented throughout the deeper parts of the sanctuary through ROV surveys. No more than six marbled grouper have been documented in one aggregation. Recent reports suggest that a possible spawning population of marbled grouper was heavily impacted by recreational fishers. Over 70 marbled grouper were extracted over a two-day period in August 2007 from neighboring Geyer Bank. This situation suggests a need to increase protection of this population during spawning periods.

Bycatch

Discarded fishing bycatch (such as dead sharks, moray eels and other non-target species) has increasingly been reported by scuba divers within the sanctuary (Figure 15). Shrimping bycatch has been illegally discarded on Stetson Bank on several occasions. Because shrimp trawls are a prohibited gear within the sanctuary, discharging material associated with shrimping is also not allowed. Impacts of discarded bycatch include smothering of benthic organisms, alteration of the bottom by the addition of shells and other materials, and unnatural attraction of sharks, rays, and other scavengers on the banks. The illegal dumping of bycatch presents a user conflict, as it could increase safety concerns for scuba divers. Unnatural feeding of marine organisms leads to increased aggression of fish, turtles, and moray eels, as the animals may associate a feeding event with deposits of "food" from the surface. This may lead to the unintentional case of mistaken identity as a diver makes an entry into the water. Injuries from barracudas have been anecdotally reported in areas where fish feeding is encouraged (Franklin Viola, pers. comm.).

Lost Gear

Lost and discarded fishing gear, including longlines, floats and nets, has been observed at East and West Flower Garden and Stetson Banks (Figure 16). Such incidents can cause localized physical injury to coral reefs, and have been documented to entangle and injure resident and transient sea turtles and other organisms. Some debris originating from prior activities, including seismic cables from acoustic surveys, remains embedded in the coral reef around the flanks of East and West Flower Garden Banks.

Spawning Aggregations

The sanctuary harbors populations of several species of snapper and grouper that may utilize areas within the sanctuary as spawning sites. On various occasions, some species (e.g., scamp, black grouper, marbled grouper) have been observed aggregating in small groups, expressing courtship and reproductive behavior. It is critical to protect these animals from focused fishing efforts during these periods. The marbled grouper is of particular concern as it is rare throughout the Gulf of Mexico and Caribbean; however, the northwestern Gulf of Mexico, in general, appears to be prime habitat for the species.

Figure 17. An invasive species, orange cup coral (*Tubastraea coccinea*).

Minerals Management Service (MMS) is part of the U.S. Department of the Interior. Its purpose is to manage the mineral resources on federal and Indian lands as well as regulate domestic energy production off America's coast on the Outer Continental Shelf. It is also responsible for collecting, verifying, and disbursing royalty revenue generated from energy production on all federal (onshore and offshore) and American Indian lands. MMS manages the Offshore Minerals Management Program and the Royalty Management Program.

Invasive Species

In 2002, an invasive coral species, *Tubastraea coccinea* (orange cup coral), was documented at East Flower Garden Bank (Figure 17). Since then, at least two other colonies have been documented. This species is native to the Indo-Pacific and may have entered the South Atlantic and Caribbean by attaching to a ship's hull, having its larvae discharged in ballast water, or being transported on a reused structure. This coral species is now common on oil and gas platforms in the Gulf of Mexico. It is suspected that artificial structures, such as oil and gas platforms, played a major role in the spread of this species. They may play a similar role for other species either through transport of the rigs and platforms themselves between locations or with their tendency to act as "stepping stones" of dispersal for species that associate with such structures. It is reasonable to anticipate the introduction of other exotic species in the future (Fenner 2004). Approximately 46 colonies of this invasive species were removed from neighboring Geyer Bank in 2005, and in March 2007, over 100 colonies were noted as thriving at the site. Also in March 2007, at least two colonies of *T. coccinea* were documented at Sonnier Bank (Ron Hill, NMFS pers. comm.).

In 2006, a pair of Pacific nudibranchs, *Thecacera pacifica*, was photographed mating at Stetson Bank. It is unknown whether this invasive species will establish a viable population, and if it does, what effect this species will have on the native fauna of Stetson.

Oil and Gas Infrastructure

Existing Structure and Maintenance

The existing platform within the Flower Garden Banks National Marine Sanctuary, designated as High Island A389A, is a fully operational natural gas production facility. In 2000, additional exploratory wells were drilled from this platform, resulting in the allowable discharge of drilling "muds" (lubricants) and cuttings shunted to within 10 meters of the sea floor. Periodic maintenance of this facility (sandblasting, painting, etc.) is required to control corrosion and ensure structural stability.

Within the Minerals Management Service (MMS) four-mile regulatory zone of both the East and West Flower Garden Banks, there are currently 15 production platforms and approximately 111 miles (179 km) of pipeline (half of which are dedicated oil pipelines). From 2004-06, three of these platforms and approximately 83 miles (134 km) of pipeline were added within the MMS four-mile regulatory zones of the East and West Flower Garden Banks. A gas pipeline has been constructed within the sanctuary near East Flower Garden Bank to connect HIA389A to a subsea station outside of the sanctuary boundaries. This pipeline is used to bring in product from the subsea station to HIA389A for processing and shipment to shore. One platform and approximately 11 miles (17.44 km) of pipeline are located within four miles (6.5 km) of Stetson Bank.

New Infrastructure

There are small areas outside the MMS "no-activity zones" but inside the sanctuary boundaries. Within these areas, the development of new oil and gas infrastructure could be considered. Development could include new platform installation, exploratory drilling and pipeline routing. A pipeline was constructed in 2004 to connect a gas well outside the sanctuary to the platform located within the sanctuary. The pipeline traverses approximately 1,000 feet (303 meters) of sanctuary habitat consisting of flat, muddy soft bottom.

Pollutant Discharge

Discharge of pollutants from sources inside and outside the sanctuary may affect sanctuary resources.

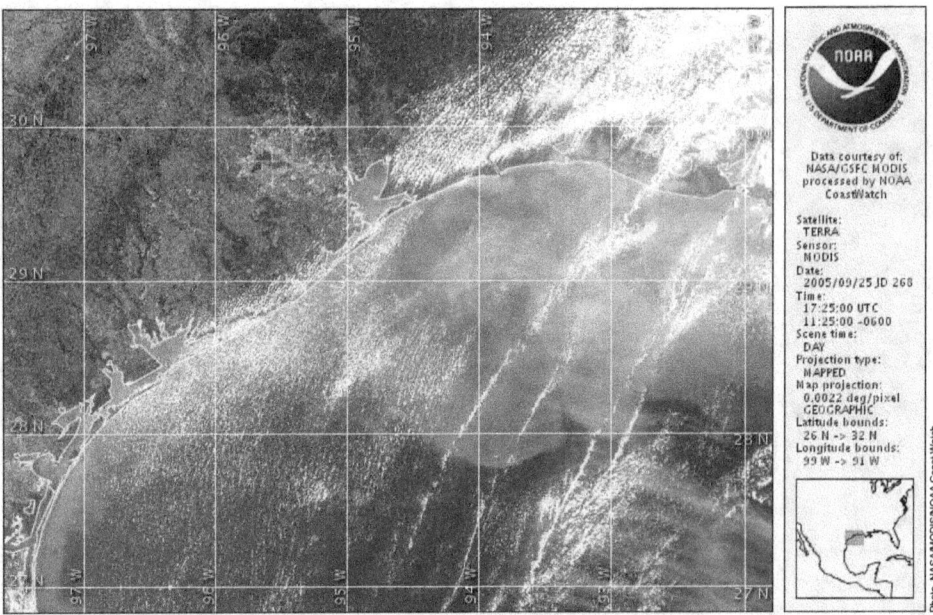

Figure 18. Satellite imagery of the plume of discolored water resulting from Hurricane Rita in August 2005.

Hydrocarbons and Associated Discharges

Impact from an oil spill or other hydrocarbon release is an ongoing concern. Major oil spills in the Gulf of Mexico are very rare, but if one did occur, it could have significant effects on the water, living resource, and habitat quality of the sanctuary. Threats to the sanctuary can result from discharges from leaking pipelines and damage to platforms (particularly resulting from natural events, such as hurricanes) or dragging of anchors. During the 2005 hurricane events, it was evident that regional response assets were severely overtaxed because of land-based and nearshore impacts. In such cases, offshore oil spills are treated as lower-priority issues, and potentially pose an elevated threat to offshore natural resources. Ongoing operational effluents from oil and gas facilities include drilling lubricants, produced water (water separated from the oil or gas after it is pumped from the reservoir), and operational discharges (sewage, graywater, deck wash).

Vessels

The discharge of untreated sewage from vessels is not allowed within the sanctuary. However, the discharge from a U.S. Coast Guard-approved marine sanitation device is currently allowed. Marine sanitation devices are only required to remove suspended solids and treat for potential human pathogens. Nutrients and other pollutants are not removed by these systems. Other vessel discharges include "graywater" from showers and galleys, deck runoff and incidental release of petrochemicals from engine use.

Coastal Runoff

The quality of coastal waters of the northern Gulf of Mexico is in decline due to pollutants associated with the discharge of major river systems (such as the Mississippi and Atchafalaya), general coastal runoff throughout the region, and habitat alteration (e.g., salt water intrusions in marshes). Predominant current patterns direct much of this water away from the sanctuary, but minor changes in circulation patterns could bring contaminated water to the sanctuary.

The 2005 hurricane events proved conclusively that the Flower Garden Banks National Marine Sanctuary is not immune to impacts from terrestrial sources. Hurricane Rita flushed the coastline of Texas and Louisiana, resulting in a persistent plume of contaminated water, which reached out and beyond the Flower Garden Banks National Marine Sanctuary and was evident for several months. It is unknown what the contaminants were in the vast plume, or what the long term effects on the reef environment will be (Figure 18).

Liquefied Natural Gas

The development of offshore liquefied natural gas (LNG) receiving terminals should be monitored in the region. LNG ports could potentially affect water quality as well as biologically important planktonic stages of fish and invertebrates critical to the continued health of the reefs and banks in the region. An "open loop" system (i.e., a system that uses seawater to warm the natural gas from its liquefied form and discharges the water directly to the surrounding waters), is located in the West Cameron Area, 35 miles (57 km) from the reef cap of East Flower Garden Bank. The Gulf Gateway Energy Bridge deepwater port is owned by Excelerate Energy Limited Partnership and has been operational since March 20, 2005.

Shipping and Transport

The sanctuary is located adjacent to a major shipping lane leading to the Port of Houston, one of the busiest ports in the nation. Historically, significant impact to coral resulted from anchoring of large ocean going vessels at the sanctuary. This impact has been minimized by the establishment of a "no-anchor" area by the International Maritime Organization (IMO) and through sanctuary regulations. However, an anchoring incident could still occur. The practice of exchanging petrochemicals between ships within nearby lightering zones could result in unintended spills. Furthermore, the release of ballast water by ships preparing to take on cargo may unintentionally introduce exotic species into the sanctuary or surrounding sensitive habitats. In the past, significant injury to sanctuary resources has also resulted from improperly attended cables between tugs and towed barges.

Visitor Use
Increasing Numbers

Visitation by scuba divers and fishermen is relatively low at present, but is expected to increase. Estimates of diver use are between 2,500 and 3,000 divers per year, resulting in a total of at least 10,000 dives annually in the sanctuary. Most of these divers arrive in one of two dive charter vessels, carrying either a maximum of 20 or 34 customers. Private vessels and researchers also visit the banks regularly. Currently, the maximum size of individual vessels allowed to use mooring buoys is 100 feet, but the number or type of vessels is not addressed.

The sanctuary is becoming internationally known as a prime dive destination, and with increased recognition will likely come higher levels of visitation. It is recognized that non-consumptive recreational diving activity may result in habitat injury, due to inappropriate physical contact with the coral reef (standing, touching, holding or accidental kicking), alteration of animal behavior (avoidance or attraction of fish species, chasing or touching marine animals), unintentional fish feeding during night dives, or other factors. Very few quantitative studies of the impact of scuba divers on coral reefs have been conducted. One study suggests that relatively low levels of scuba diving activity (less than 6,000 divers per year) have minimal impact on coral reefs (Hawkins et al. 1999). Coral reefs in other parts of the world have experienced degradation associated with intense visitor use, especially by snorkelers in very shallow (less than 3 meters deep) reef zones (Allison 2005). It has also been proposed that divers may act as vec-

tors for some types of coral disease by the use of dive gear that has been contaminated while diving in areas with high incidence of coral disease and then not properly disinfected (Marano-Briggs 2006).

The level of recreational and commercial fishing is not precisely known at the Flower Garden Banks. Reports by long-time users of the sanctuary and observations by sanctuary staff and others suggest that the level of fishing activity has been increasing in recent years. Stetson Bank is heavily used during mackerel season, and fishermen target wahoo aggregations, which are currently without catch limits, at the East and West Flower Garden Banks. Local fishers report that it is necessary to travel farther offshore in recent years to find certain species (red snapper, grouper, etc.) compared to in the past (J. Stout, pers. comm.). Large commercial charter fishing vessels ("headboats") have been observed regularly at Stetson Bank, and smaller fishing charters offer trips to the Flower Garden Banks. As noted above, technological advances in vessel design and equipment have made it easier to find and catch fish.

User Conflicts

As interest and use in the sanctuary increases, there will potentially be conflicts among users arising from competing objectives. As an example, recreational fishermen and dive charters may compete for use of the same reef areas. Typically, recreational fishers target the same types of large fish that divers travel to the sanctuary to see. In addition, fishing in an area where diving is occurring can pose a potential safety risk. This type of user conflict is occurring at the current user level, especially at Stetson Bank, and can be expected to intensify as the number of users increases.

Fish Feeding

Fishing and shrimping vessels have been discarding bycatch in sanctuary waters while tied to mooring buoys, and private vessels visiting the sanctuary have been observed depositing food scraps into the water.

Mooring Buoys

As the number of users increases, it is anticipated that competition for mooring buoys will increase. Use of the mooring buoys is currently guided by a "first-come, first-served" policy, which could lead to conflicts without additional installations. It could also lead to maintenance or safety concerns as vessels begin to tie in tandem to existing buoys, causing excessive strain on the mooring system.

Wildlife Interactions
Physical Contact

The experience of swimming and diving with large charismatic animals is one of many attractions of the sanctuary. However, physical

Figure 19. Divers riding a manta ray. This activity is strongly discouraged, as it can put both the diver and manta ray at risk of being injured.

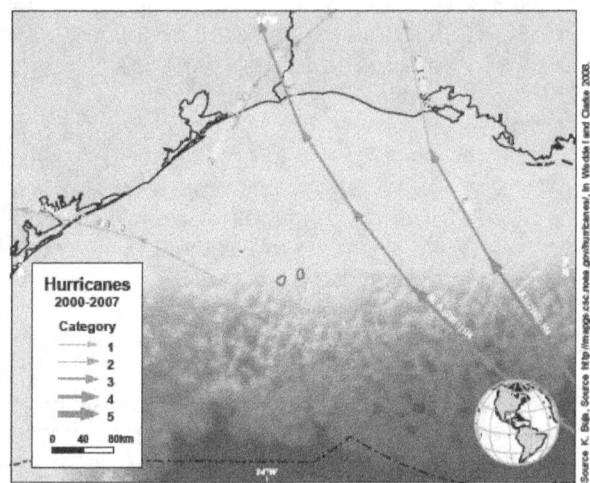

Figure 20. Map showing the paths and intensities of tropical storms passing near the Flower Garden Banks National Marine Sanctuary and nearby banks from 2000 - 2007.

contact with animals, such as whale sharks, manta rays (Figure 19), and sea turtles, may alter the animal's behavior and have other undocumented impacts that should be investigated. Physical contact with sea turtles, which are on the endangered and threatened species lists, is already prohibited, but other large marine animals are not as strictly protected. In the past, changes in behavior of some animals subject to physical contact have been observed. In one case, a diver riding a manta ray (a strongly discouraged activity) inadvertently forced it to collide with the reef, putting both the diver and the manta ray at risk.

Underwater Sound

Over the past three decades, the sanctuary has been subjected to increasing sources of underwater sounds, the effects of which are poorly understood. These sources include boat engines and generators, as well as commercial, experimental and exploration activities, the most prominent being acoustic air gun surveys, pile driving, and work boat transits associated with the oil and gas industry. As far as we know, no sounds occur at levels considered detrimental to sanctuary resources, but concerns have been expressed about the cumulative impacts of these sounds. These impacts could include altering feeding or mating behaviors or causing animals to avoid areas they would otherwise occupy (Pearson et al. 1992, Engas et al. 1996).

Light

There is some evidence that unnatural nighttime levels of artificial light from dive vessels and other sources have altered the behavior of some marine animals on the reef. For example, barracudas and other predators aggregate around illuminated vessels at night to feed on smaller fish attracted to the lights. Intense light from underwater photography and video by divers has been observed to alter the behavior of sea turtles and other species. In addition, sea turtles and fish can be awakened during nightly resting periods and clearly disturbed by dive lights, flood lights and strobes. Dive lights often allow predators, such as dog snappers (*Lutjanus jocu*) and black jacks (*Caranx lugubris*), to prey on smaller reef fish as they trail scuba divers at night.

Hurricanes

The Flower Garden Banks have been in the path of numerous tropical storms and hurricanes (Figure 20). In 2005, two powerful hurricanes illustrated that the reefs of the sanctuary are not immune to the force of these storms. The eye of Hurricane Rita passed within 30 miles (48 km) of East Flower Garden Bank, resulting in coral heads as large as 13 feet (4 meters) in diameter being overturned and transported. Enormous barrel sponges were sheared off, and sand patches were scoured. Some fields of delicate pencil coral (*Madracis mirabilis*) at East Flower Garden Bank were severely impacted. Sections of Stetson Bank pinnacles were sheared off, and valleys were scoured clean. Impacts were documented by researchers as deep as 250 feet (76 meters) in the brine seep at East Flower Garden Bank (K. Parsons-Hubbard, pers. comm.). Impacts from the 2005 hurricane event continued to be visible in July 2007.

State of Sanctuary Resources

This section provides summaries of the conditions and trends within four resource areas: water, habitat, living resources and maritime archaeological resources. For each, sanctuary staff and selected outside experts considered a series of questions about each resource area. The set of questions is derived from the National Marine Sanctuary System's mission, and a system-wide monitoring framework (National Marine Sanctuary Program 2004) developed to ensure the timely flow of data and information to those responsible for managing and protecting resources in the ocean and coastal zone, and to those that use, depend on, and study the ecosystems encompassed by the sanctuaries. The questions are meant to set the limits of judgments so that responses can be confined to certain reporting categories that will later be compared among all sanctuary sites and combined. The appendix (Rating Scheme for System-Wide Monitoring Questions) clarifies the set of questions and presents statements that were used to judge the status and assign a corresponding color code on a scale from "good" to "poor." These statements are customized for each question. In addition, the following options are available for all questions: "N/A" — the question does not apply; and "undetermined" – resource status is undetermined. In addition, symbols are used to indicate trends: "▲" - conditions appear to be improving; "—" - conditions do not appear to be changing; "▼" - conditions appear to be declining; and "?" - the trend is undetermined.

This section of the report provides answers to the set of questions. Answers are supported by specific examples of data, investigations, monitoring and observations, and the basis for judgment is provided in the text and summarized in the table for each resource area. Where published or additional information exists, the reader is provided with appropriate references and Web links.

Water

1. Are specific or multiple stressors, including changing oceanographic and atmospheric conditions, affecting water quality and how are they changing? Because selected conditions, such as isolated contaminants, freshwater influxes from terrestrial sources, and increased water temperature, have been shown to affect living resource assemblages and habitats to some extent, this question is rated "good/fair and declining."

Recent events of coral bleaching (2005 in particular) are the result of higher-than-normal seawater temperature extremes (Precht et al. In press). Further, hourly in situ water measurements taken at the East and West Flower Garden Banks reflected higher-than-average temperatures in 2005, which deviated from the mean temperature more in winter months than in the summer. Preliminary data (Precht et al. In press) indicate that the increased water temperatures are more pronounced at West Flower Garden Bank than at the East Flower Garden Bank.

Climate change could certainly affect resources in the sanctuary, particularly as a result of temperature stress or ocean acidification. The recent warm water events (Precht et al. In press) have affected corals to some extent, but there is not yet persistent enough evidence of warming to conclude that climate change effects are yet being exhibited in this sanctuary. This is an area of monitoring that will need to be addressed in the future.

Influxes of fresh water originating from land-based or river sources may contribute to the introduction of pollutants of terrestrial origin including pesticides and fertilizers, and cause lower salinity conditions, all of which can contribute to decreased water quality. Freshwater lenses have been recorded by in situ measurements in the months of June, July, and August at the East and West Flower Garden Banks, but extend through September and October at Stetson Bank. It is noted that this freshwater lens does not appear to extend deeper than around 33–50 feet (10–15 meters) depth, although in some cases the associated low water quality could inhibit light reaching the substrate (Deslarzes and Lugo-Fernández 2007).

Contaminants also originate from discharges from oil and gas platform operations. The exact contaminants contained in produced water are highly variable and difficult to track accurately. It is known that heavy metals, such as lead, cadmium, mercury and radioactive compounds, are associated with oil and gas activities in some circumstances. Studies have shown that the sediments surrounding the gas production platform known as High Island A389A, located within the sanctuary boundaries, contain comparatively high levels of mercury, lead, cadmium, zinc and other contaminants, probably due to the stipulations that require drilling lubricants and cuttings be shunted to within 10 meters of the seabed to avoid creating a sediment plume that could envelope the shallow reef areas (Kennicutt et al. 1995).

2. What is the eutrophic condition of sanctuary waters and how is it changing? Nutrient measurements have been made on numerous occasions beginning in the late 1980s as part of the regularly scheduled long-term monitoring program (Gittings and

Boland 1991, Gittings et al. 1992b, Continental Shelf Assoc. 1996, Dokken et al. 1999, Dokken et al. 2003, Precht et al. In press). None of the measurements suggest an increasing threat of eutrophication, therefore, the rating for this question is "good and not changing."

3. *Do sanctuary waters pose risks to human health and how are they changing?* Because of recent outbreaks of cigua-

tera that have been traced to fish from the Flower Garden Banks, and because a large proportion of fish tested for mercury exceeded levels for safe consumption, this question is rated "fair/poor and declining."

Taylor (1973) found concentrations of mercury in barracuda (*Sphyraena barracuda*) to be as high as 1.82 ppm in muscle tissue and 0.56 ppm in liver. In 2002, samples of five barracuda assessed for mercury levels were above EPA levels for cause for

FDA Advisory Zones

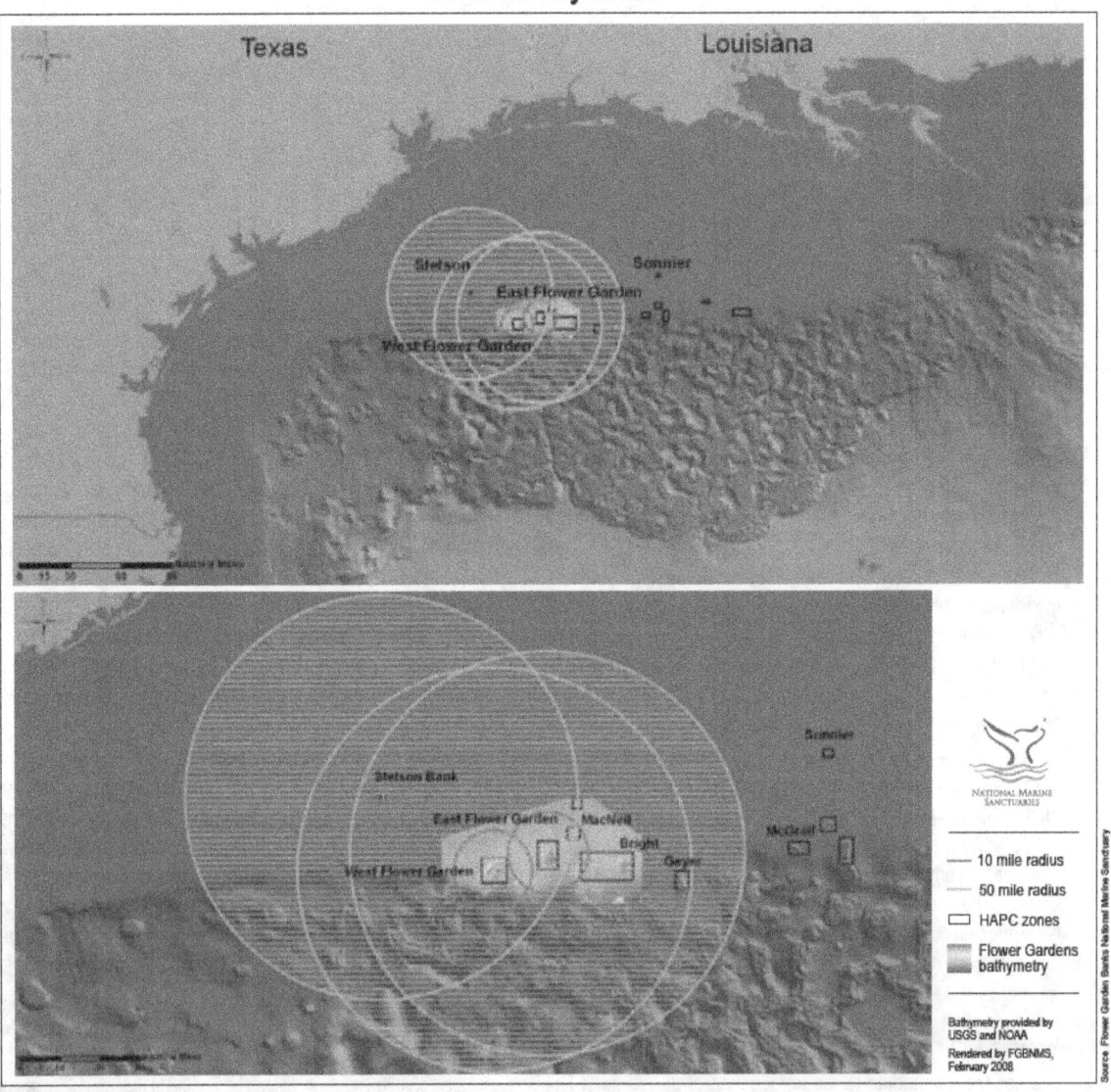

Figure 21. FDA advisory zones that were issued in response to concern over a number of recent outbreaks of ciguatera fish poisoning.

concern (0.3 ppm; Marc Engel, State of Florida). In 2007, 24 of 31 analyzed fish had mercury levels at or above that level (David Evans, NOAA/National Centers for Coastal Ocean Science).

Dr. Tracy Villareal (University of Texas Marine Science Institute) reported the first encounter of the toxic dinoflagellate *Gambierdiscus toxicus* in algae sampled at the Flower Garden Banks in September 2006. At that time it was unknown whether ciguatoxins were entering the food web of the sanctuary. Villareal et al. (2007) reported that the increased substrate availability provided by the oil and gas industry in the Gulf of Mexico has contributed to the increased levels of ciguatoxins regionally, leading to increased incidents of ciguatera poisoning. In April 2007, the Galveston Daily News reported that two individuals from Galveston, Texas, had suffered from ciguatera poisoning after consuming a grouper caught in the Flower Garden Banks National Marine Sanctuary. The fish was later identified as a gag grouper. Analysis by Bob Dickey (U.S. Food and Drug Administration) confirmed that the fish tested positive for ciguatoxin.

In response to this event, sanctuary staff collaborated with Villareal, Dickey, Patricia Hay and Quay Dortch (NCCOS), to obtain and analyze fish samples. A vessel was provided by John Stout, a recreational fishing member of the Flower Garden Banks National Marine Sanctuary Advisory Committee, and funding was provided by NOAA for the cruise response. On June 5, 2007, 31 fish were collected and provided to the FDA and NCCOS for analysis. In addition to the analysis for ciguatoxin levels, the fish were aged by Dr. Linda Lombardi-Carlson (NMFS/SEFSC, Panama City), and mercury levels were analyzed by Dr. David Evans (NCCOS).

Four of the 31 fish tested positive for elevated levels of ciguatoxin — a marbled grouper (*Dermatolepis inermis*), scamp grouper (*Mycteroperca phenax*), barracuda (*Sphyraena barracuda*) and sand tilefish (*Malacanthus plumieri*).

On Feb. 5, 2008, the FDA issued an advisory targeting seafood processors purchasing grouper, amberjack, and related predatory reef species captured in the northern Gulf of Mexico (Figure 21). The advisory was issued in response to the FDA's concern over a number of recent outbreaks of ciguatera fish poisoning that had been traced to fish from the vicinity of the sanctuary. The FDA considers ciguatera fish poisoning a likely hazard for hogfish, grouper and snapper species of concern captured within 10 miles of the sanctuary, and amberjack, barracuda and other pelagic species of concern captured within 50 miles of the sanctuary. FDA officials recommended that primary processors avoid purchasing the listed species from the area detailed. To download the full advisory, visit http://www.regulations.gov/ and search for FDA-2008-D-0079-0002.

4. What are the levels of human activities that may influence water quality and how are they changing?

Discharges from numerous sources influence water quality at the Flower Garden Banks National Marine Sanctuary. These include recreational dive charter vessels, recreational and commercial fishing vessels, transiting oil and gas tankers and other ship traffic. Other sources include discharge from oil and gas platforms associated with exploration, development and production facilities. The levels of these activities appear to be stable and significant impacts have not been documented, therefore, this question is rated "good/fair and not changing." Oil and gas development activities fluctuate over time due to market conditions and other factors. It is anticipated that within the next 5-10 years many platforms in this region of the Gulf of Mexico will be decommissioned, resulting in short-term increased activity in the vicinity. However, levels of fishing appear to be increasing in and around the sanctuary (though the recent FDA advisory on fish consumption may change this, at least in the short term).

Water Quality Status & Trends

#	Issue	Rating	Basis for Judgment	Description of Findings
1	Stressors	▼	Isolated contaminants; freshwater influxes from terrestrial sources; increased water temperature.	Selected conditions may preclude full development of living resource assemblages and habitats, but are not likely to cause substantial or persistent declines.
2	Eutrophic Condition	–	No evidence based on ongoing monitoring since the late 1980s.	Conditions do not appear to have the potential to negatively affect living resources or habitat quality.
3	Human Health	▼	Recent outbreaks of ciguatera traced to fish from the Flower Gardens; large proportion of fish tested for mercury exceeded levels for safe consumption.	Selected conditions have caused or are likely to cause severe impacts, but cases to date have not suggested a pervasive problem.
4	Human Activities	–	Vessel discharges, oil and gas platform and pipeline discharges.	Some potentially harmful activities exist, but they do not appear to have had a negative effect on water quality.

Status: | Good | Good/Fair | Fair | Fair/Poor | Poor | Undet. |

Trends: Improving (▲), Not Changing (–), Getting Worse (▼), Undetermined Trend (?), Question not applicable (N/A)

Habitat

5. *What are the abundance and distribution of major habitat types and how are they changing?* The abundance and distribution of major habitat types in the sanctuary is considered to be "good and not changing." With over 50% living coral coverage the Flower Garden Banks is considered to be one of the healthiest reef systems in the Caribbean (Lang et al. 2001). Monitoring data collected since the 1970s indicate no significant changes in the nature of habitats on the coral reefs, with short-term exceptions being those caused by the die-off of many *Diadema antillarum* sea urchins in 1983-84, and mechanical damage caused by certain human activities such as anchoring (Gittings 1998). The sea urchin die-off resulted in high leafy algae cover that persisted for about a year, but no measured loss in coral cover. Several anchoring incidents have resulted in damage at the Flower Garden Banks, most leaving toppled, fractured and abraded corals (Gittings et al. 1997). Anchor damage in deep habitats on the banks has not been measured directly, though evidence of disturbance can be seen on side-scan and multi-beam images of the seafloor. Isolated damage has also been caused by tow cable drags, one of which affected individual coral colonies along a path of about 300 meters. Though scars persisted for many years, most corals affected by these incidents survived and healed.

Habitat impacts were caused by Hurricane Rita in 2005, which passed within 30 miles (48 km) of the sanctuary. Considerable sand movement and toppling of numerous large coral colonies were evident (Robbart et al. In press). Fields of *Madracis mirabilis* suffered extensive damage as a result of the hurricane. Mechanical damage continued to be visible in July 2007. These natural changes have been seen in previous hurricanes (e.g., Hurricane Allen in 1980) and reef organisms appear to recover from these impacts if they are not too severe.

6. *What is the condition of biologically structured habitats and how is it changing?* Long-term monitoring suggests that coral-dominated habitats are in "good/fair" condition, as numerous human activities have affected portions of the otherwise thriving coral reef. Coral cover and growth rates have been nearly the same for decades (Figure 22) (Gittings and Bo-

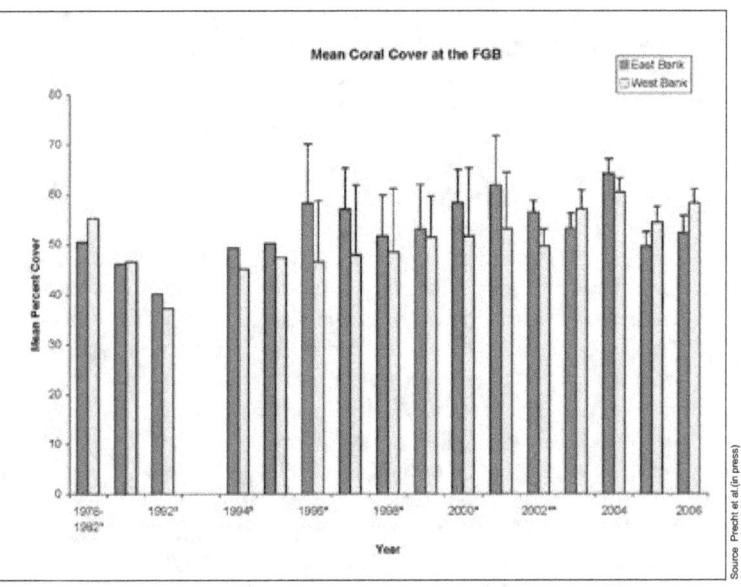

Figure 22. Coral cover from 1998 – 2006. Compiled from: Kraemer (1982) 1978-1982; Gittings (1998) 1988-1991; Continental Shelf Associates (1996) 1994-1995; Dokken et al. (2003) 1996-2001 with standard deviations; PBS&J 2002 - present with standard errors.

land 1991, Gittings et al. 1992c, Continental Shelf Assoc. 1996, Dokken et al. 1999, Dokken et al. 2003, Precht et al. In press). Nevertheless, some habitat disturbance and loss has resulted from fishing gear (nets, longlines and monofilament line) entanglement, seismic cable entanglement, anchoring, and cable dragging. Also, discarded industry equipment such as pipes has been encountered during ROV surveys.

A major coral bleaching event in 2005 resulted in the loss of approximately 1 percent (Robbart et al. In press) of the fire coral (*Millepora alcicornis*). Bleaching has been documented in the past (Hagman and Gittings 1992), but mortality was minimal. It is uncertain whether recent bleaching events are evidence of increasing severity in general or simply isolated severe events. It appears that fire coral at Stetson Bank suffered mortality during the 2005 season due to increased water temperature. Data analysis is currently underway to verify these observations.

Also at Stetson Bank, observations of fragmented rock outcrops suggest that fishing gear or anchoring—possibly both—have caused their destruction. The claystone outcrops on Stetson Bank are very fragile compared to those on coral reefs, which are a form of limestone. At Stetson Bank, corals and sponges grow in abundance on these outcrops, but when fishing gear or anchors snag on the features, both the living organisms and the rocks themselves can be destroyed. The rock itself, in breaking loose, becomes more susceptible to movement and therefore less suitable for invertebrate recruitment and survival.

7. *What are the contaminant concentrations in sanctuary habitats and how are they changing?* Limited investigations have not shown any contaminants within the coral reef zone. Therefore, the rating for this question is "good." Because there are limited investigations to date, a trend is "undetermined." Numerous contaminants have been documented in sediments (discharged drill cuttings and lubricants) below the gas production platform, (HIA389A) at depths of 400 feet (120 meters) within the sanctuary, but they are very localized and do not appear to have the potential to affect resources on East Flower Garden Bank itself (Kennicutt et al.1995).

8. *What are the levels of human activities that may influence habitat quality and how are they changing?* Because some potentially harmful activities exist in the sanctuary this question is rated "good/fair and not changing." One recreational dive charter operator is currently operating, running trips with two vessels to the sanctuary, each with a carrying capacity of 20–34 customers. Approximately 2,500-3,000 divers visit the sanctuary each year, making a total of at least 10,000 dives in the sanctuary. The level of diving activity has not changed substantially in recent years.

The level of private, charter and commercial fishing is not well documented, but appears to be increasing. Discarded fishing gear and injured or dead fish, moray eels and sharks have been documented. A spear gun was recently found at East Flower Garden Bank, and spear tips have been recovered from all three banks, indicating that prohibited activities are taking place. Longline fishing is illegal within the sanctuary, as is bottom trawling, yet longline gear is often encountered during ROV operations in deeper waters, as are discarded trawl nets. Active longline fishing within the sanctuary boundaries has been witnessed by dive charter operators.

Artificial reef program activities should be monitored for potential impacts to sanctuary resources, as well as other important biological reefs and banks in the region. With the expectation that a large number of oil and gas platforms in the northwestern Gulf of Mexico will be retired in the next 10 years, there will be pressure for an increasing level of "reefing" of oil and gas structures in the area. Impacts could include the addition of non-native species, which could harbor exotic diseases and parasites. The development of fish aquaculture using artificial

Habitat Status & Trends

#	Issue	Rating	Basis for Judgment	Description of Findings
5	Abundance/ Distribution	—	Major habitat types appear to be stable, although additional monitoring in deeper communities is warranted.	Habitats are in pristine or near-pristine condition and are unlikely to preclude full community development.
6	Structure	—	Damage by anchoring; lost or discarded fishing gear and cables, mostly in deep habitats; destabilization by fishing gear and/or anchors at Stetson Bank.	Selected habitat loss or alteration has taken place, precluding full development of living resources, but it is unlikely to cause substantial or persistent degradation in living resources or water quality.
7	Contaminants	?	Limited investigations suggest low levels of contaminants.	Contaminants do not appear to have the potential to negatively affect living resources or water quality.
8	Human Activities	—	Limited number of dive charters, some fishing gear impacts, some illegal fishing.	Some potentially harmful activities exist, but they do not appear to have had a negative effect on habitat quality.

Status: | Good | Good/Fair | Fair | Fair/Poor | Poor | Undet. |

Trends: Improving (▲), Not Changing (—), Getting Worse (▼), Undetermined Trend (?), Question not applicable (N/A)

structures such as platforms is being actively investigated and, if implemented, may affect the sanctuary area in the near future.

Living Resources

9. *What is the status of biodiversity and how is it changing?* Data collected as part of the long-term monitoring program at the Flower Garden Banks indicate that in most respects, the coral reef community is stable, including living coral cover, species dominance and diversity, and growth rates (Gittings and Boland 1991, Gittings et al. 1992b, Continental Shelf Assoc. 1996, Dokken et al. 1999, Dokken et al. 2003, Precht et al. In press). For this reason, the status of biodiversity in the sanctuary is considered to be "good and not changing." As mentioned above, some loss of fire coral cover occurred after the 2005 bleaching event. The research team and partners from academic institutions, consulting firms, and non-profit organizations (e.g., Reef Environmental Education Foundation) continue to add to the species known within the sanctuary as more observations are made. The Mardi Gras wrasse, a new species of wrasse described in 2007, appears to be thriving at Stetson Bank.

10. What is the status of environmentally sustainable fishing and how is it changing? No directed studies have occurred to address this question, though they are clearly needed in both shallow and deep areas of the sanctuary to assess rates of removal and impacts to the food web. Anecdotal reports from experienced observers, including numerous researchers and recreational divers, suggest a decline in the number of large fish (principally groupers and jacks). Also, lower numbers of large pelagic sharks, primarily the scalloped hammerhead, have been observed during the winter months in recent years. For these reasons, the status of environmentally sustainable fishing is considered to be "fair," though the trend is "undetermined."

11. What is the status of non-indigenous species and how is it changing? Some non-indigenous species exist in the sanctuary, but they are sparse enough to preclude substantial or persistent degradation to the ecosystem. Therefore, this question is rated "good/fair". Three colonies of an Indo-Pacific species of orange cup coral (*Tubastraea coccinea*) have been found in the sanctuary. This species may be becoming better established in the region. Prior to this finding, the coral had been reported in the Gulf of Mexico, but primarily on artificial structures such as oil and gas platforms. *Tubastraea* is thriving on HIA389A, but has only recently been documented at East Flower Garden Bank (1 mile from the platform). No colonies have been reported at West Flower Garden Bank. On neighboring Geyer Bank, nearly 50 colonies of *Tubastraea* were removed by sanctuary research divers in 2004. Over 100 colonies were observed at Geyer Bank during surveys in 2007. *Tubastraea* appears to be an aggressive colonizer, and sanctuary leadership has decided to remove it from the reef when it is encountered.

A Pacific species of nudibranch (*Thecacera pacifica*) was recently documented at Stetson Bank. It was photographed during reproduction, so it is likely that this species is becoming established. It is unknown how this species will impact the Stetson Bank ecosystem.

12. What is the status of key species and how is it changing? Because substantial changes have been observed, both in the long term and in recent years, for certain key species in the Flower Garden Banks sanctuary, the status overall is rated at "good/fair." But because rates of change and recovery have not been adequately

assessed, the trend is rated as "undetermined." Monitoring results indicate that coral populations are stable, although there is some concern about the potential effects of the apparent emergence of diseases that affect them (Gittings and Boland 1991, Gittings et al. 1992b, Continental Shelf Assoc. 1996, Dokken et al. 1999, Dokken et al. 2003, Precht et al. In press). Based on frequent but non-quantified observations by sanctuary staff and others, abundance of hammerhead sharks, groupers and jacks appears to be lower than a decade or so ago. Sea turtle, manta ray and whale shark populations appear to be stable, though their numbers fluctuate annually. Whale shark encounters remain unpredictable, so changes in their abundance are difficult to assess. Long-spined sea urchins (*Diadema antillarum*), which many consider an important keystone species on Caribbean reefs, experienced almost complete mortality at the Flower Garden Banks in 1983-84, and remain in low abundance. Interestingly, *Diadema* are more abundant at Stetson Bank, and populations at West Flower Garden Bank are increasing slowly. There is a lack of information on species in deep habitats, particularly groupers, jacks and snappers that inhabit those areas.

13. What is the condition or health of key species and how is it changing? Coral growth rates, levels of fecundity (based on observations during mass spawning events), and other indices of coral vitality appear to be comparable to those observed since the banks were first studied (Gittings and Boland 1991, Gittings et al. 1992c, Continental Shelf Assoc. 1996, Dokken et al. 1999, Dokken et al. 2003, Precht et al. In press). Coral spawning at the Flower Garden Banks National Marine Sanctuary continues to be one of the most prolific and predictable events in the Caribbean, and the few recruitment studies (Baggett 1985, Snell et al. 1998, Hagman 2001) conducted suggest good conditions and levels of recruitment of coral larvae. However, recent ephemeral outbreaks of coral disease, which has resulted in tissue loss on affected colonies, and the 2005 coral bleaching event suggest that the health of key species may be less than optimal. The bleaching event was severe, and there was measurable loss of fire coral (*Millepora alcicornis*). For this reason, the condition of key species in the sanctuary is considered to be "good/fair and declining."

In winter 2005, the first significant documented coral disease outbreak at the Flower Garden Banks occurred, affecting multiple coral species and numerous colonies. Repeat occurrences of this plague-like event happened in the winters of 2006, 2007 and 2008.

These events have been unusual, as typical coral disease events elsewhere are more severe during warmer water temperatures. The Flower Garden Banks coral disease events have, to date, been active during the winter months, and declined significantly as water temperatures increased. No overall decrease in coral cover has been documented as a result of these disease events through the long-term monitoring program; however, tissue loss on individual affected coral colonies has been documented, and gives cause for concern over the long term (Precht et al. In press).

Sea turtles appear to be in good health, based on body size and mass, as do the manta rays, grouper and sharks found in the sanctuary. Some whale sharks, however, show signs of vessel strikes (scars and gouges on their bodies and fins).

14. *What are the levels of human activities that may influence living resource quality and how are they changing?* The most common and persistent human activities occurring at the Flower Garden Banks are diving and fishing, but other activities, such as anchoring by large vessels and dragging of tow cables, occasionally occur. All these activities can cause measurable impacts to habitats and living resources, but evidence to date suggests effects are localized, not widespread. Thus, this status is rated "fair".

The levels of recreational diving activities appear stable, though at present, the sanctuary does not have a system in place to fully monitor diving activity. A new dive operator has indicated their intention to begin a charter at the Flower Garden Banks, so levels may increase. It is important to estimate the carrying capacity of the reef and implement a system to evaluate the numbers of visitors to the reef. Also, it may become necessary to rotate buoys used by recreational divers if localized impacts are shown to result from heavy use of moorings.

No formal reporting process is in place to evaluate recreational and commercial fishing use at the sanctuary, therefore, the trend rating for this question is "undetermined." Observations by long-time users and sanctuary staff indicate elevated visitation by recreational fisherman at all three banks in the sanctuary. Levels of commercial fishing are not well known, but investigations following the recent outbreak of ciguatera originating in fish from the banks suggest that a considerable number of commercial fish, including some that are quite rare throughout their range (i.e., marbled grouper), are taken from deep habitats at the Flower Garden Banks.

Living Resources Status & Trends

#	Issue	Rating	Basis for Judgment	Description of Findings
9	Biodiversity	–	Long-term monitoring of coral reef communities and other information collected since the 1970s.	Biodiversity appears to reflect pristine or near-pristine conditions and promotes ecosystem integrity (full community development and function).
10	Extracted Species	?	Unpublished observations suggest a decline in certain species of fish, e.g. grouper and jacks.	Extraction may inhibit full community development and function and may cause measurable but not severe degradation of ecosystem integrity.
11	Non-Indigenous Species	–	Recent invasive species have been discovered, but abundances are low and there is no evidence that they have become established in natural areas.	Non-indigenous species exist, precluding full community development and function, but are unlikely to cause substantial or persistent degradation of ecosystem integrity.
12	Key Species Status	?	Coral, mantas and sea turtles appear to be stable. Hammerhead, grouper, snapper, and jacks may be declining. *Diadema* sea urchin populations remain depressed since the 1983-84 die-off.	Selected key or keystone species are at reduced levels, perhaps precluding full community development and function, but substantial or persistent declines are not expected.
13	Key Species Condition	▼	Observations of coral disease for four straight years, though no apparent population impact to date; loss of some *Millepora alcicornis* due to bleaching.	The condition of selected key resources is not optimal, perhaps precluding full ecological function, but substantial or persistent declines are not expected.
14	Human Activities	?	Stable levels of recreational diving, apparent increase and effectiveness of private and commercial fishing; no monitoring of use levels is in place.	Selected activities have resulted in measurable living resource impacts, but evidence suggests effects are localized, not widespread.

Status: | Good | Good/Fair | Fair | Fair/Poor | Poor | Undet. |

Trends: Improving (▲), Not Changing (—), Getting Worse (▼), Undetermined Trend (?), Question not applicable (**N/A**)

Maritime Archaeological Resources

Although no significant maritime archaeological artifacts have been identified in the Flower Garden Banks National Marine Sanctuary, regulations prohibit the removal, damage, or disturbance of any historical or cultural resource within the boundaries of the sanctuary. Several fluked anchors have been observed during ROV surveys. These anchors could be 100 years old based on the design of the flukes.

Maritime Archaeological Resources Status & Trends

#	Issue	Rating	Basis for Judgment	Description of Findings
15	Integrity	N/A	No documented underwater archeological sites.	N/A
16	Threat to Environment	N/A	No documented underwater archeological sites.	N/A
17	Human Activities	N/A	No documented underwater archeological sites.	N/A

Status: | Good | Good/Fair | Fair | Fair/Poor | Poor | Undet. |

Trends: Improving (▲), Not Changing (—), Getting Worse (▼), Undetermined Trend (**?**), Question not applicable (**N/A**)

Response to Pressures

The Flower Gardens Banks National Marine Sanctuary, like other marine sanctuaries, is managed using an "adaptive" management approach to resource protection, wherein threats are addressed when they are identified and understood. Adaptive management is a structured, iterative process of decision making, with the aim of reducing uncertainty over time via system monitoring and management plan updates. Adaptive management recognizes that management is an iterative learning exercise rather than a predetermined "solution" to an identified problem (Marshall and Schuttenberg 2006). The periodic review of the sanctuary's management plan, including the development of specific action plans to address priority issues, provide a mechanism to apply adaptive management techniques to problems at the Flower Garden Banks.

This report identifies a number of issues that may indicate early signs of deterioration of the coral ecosystem in the Flower Garden Banks National Marine Sanctuary. Some of these issues require more research to fully understand the problems and identify potential management actions to mitigate the impacts. However, it is important that, where appropriate, management options be considered as soon as possible, before changes become irreversible. Existing management activities that relate to the pressures and recent concerns identified in this report are highlighted below.

Aquaculture and Artificial Reefs

The monitoring program at the Flower Garden Banks is designed to track some of the potential impacts of aquaculture and artificial reefs. Fish and invertebrate monitoring techniques employed on the banks are efficient at recognizing non-indigenous species even at low abundance. Unfortunately, the methods do not document changes in conditions that could be caused by changing levels of parasitism or disease resulting from interactions with aquaculture facilities. Should such facilities be placed near the sanctuary, it will be essential for the relevant authorities to require operators to monitor water quality and minimize the scale and extent of impacts to surrounding environments.

One possible effect of artificial reefs, according to Villareal et al. (2007), is the proliferation of the dinoflagellate that causes ciguatera poisoning in fish. In this regard, artificial reefs and petroleum platforms may work together to exacerbate the problem. Research remains to determine the extent to which this and other processes affect levels of ciguatera in the Flower Gardens Banks National Marine Sanctuary.

Current Minerals Management Service (MMS) guidelines require the removal of production platforms within a year of cessation of lease-block activity. The gas production facility in the Flower Garden Banks, and several others nearby, may go off-line in the next five to 10 years. Decisions on the fate of these facilities near the sanctuary have not been made, but sanctuary staff will engage in discussions with the operators and the MMS to ensure that acceptable solutions are found.

Climate Change

Warming oceans have been linked to increasing levels and frequency of coral bleaching throughout the world's oceans. The reefs of the Flower Garden Banks are not immune to these events, and therefore the sanctuary supports regular monitoring to detect the occurrence and extent of bleaching. When incidents are reported, scientists collect information on the degree and impacts. By tracking coral bleaching from year to year, sanctuary staff can recognize events, identify related phenomena (e.g., hurricane-induced coastal runoff or anomalous temperature conditions) and take steps to reduce further impacts to the reef.

Temperature measurements have been made at the Flower Garden Banks for over 30 years. By itself, the information is insufficient to determine whether global warming is, as yet, affecting sanctuary resources directly. But data will continue to be gathered and made available to the larger ocean science community in order to contribute to our understanding of global climate change.

The sanctuary staff works to reduce other impacts and stressors in order to maximize reef community resistance and resilience in light of impending changes in climatic conditions, which the sanctuary cannot control. Recognizing that coral reef decline is typically due to the cumulative impacts of multiple stressors, management strategies should be directed at those potential impacts that can be controlled, thereby lessening the effects of climate change (Marshall and Schuttenberg 2006).

Coral Disease

The sanctuary staff regularly monitors the incidence and severity of coral disease at the Flower Garden Banks. Sanctuary staff sponsors regular research expeditions to the banks and, since the initial documentation of disease in 2005, has invited specialists in coral disease to conduct surveys and assessments during and after disease outbreaks. Current regulations prohibit the transport of corals or other organisms from other locations to the Flower Garden Banks, primarily because of the potential for disease introduction. There are currently no plans in place for treating or removing diseased animals from the sanctuary, but research is encouraged in order to identify

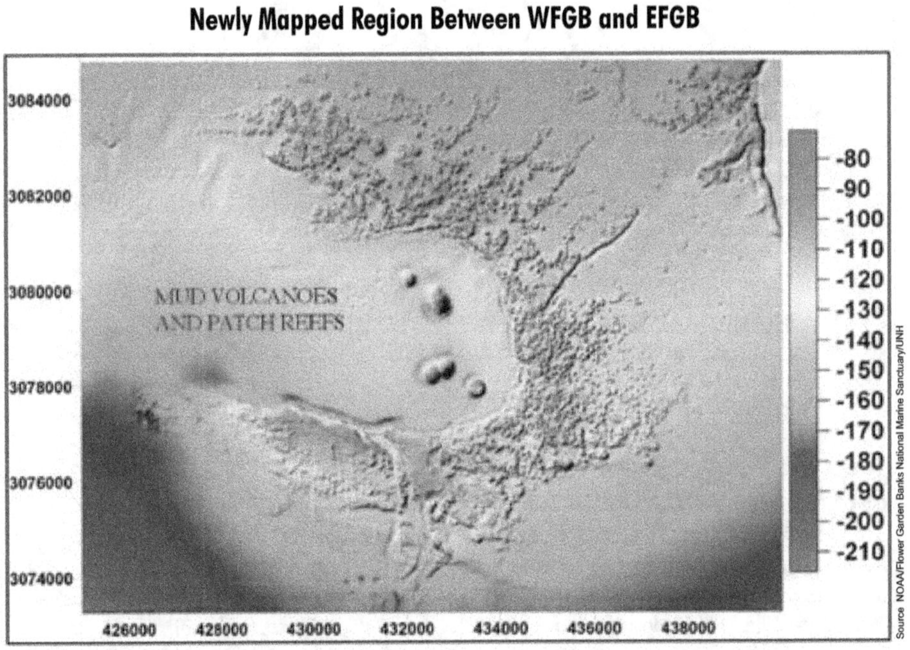

Newly Mapped Region Between WFGB and EFGB

Figure 23. High-resolution bathymetry of Horseshoe Bank, located between East and West Flower Garden Banks.

the responsible disease pathogens. If a disease pathogen is related to a human-associated source, management actions may be appropriate to mitigate further introduction. It has been suggested, for example, that coral disease may be introduced via contaminated gear used by divers who had visited diseased areas. Preventative actions requiring disinfection of dive gear could eventually be considered at the Flower Garden Banks if this theory is proven.

Significant Regional Habitat

Original sanctuary boundaries were established without the benefit of detailed bathymetric mapping of the surrounding areas. Recently produced maps demonstrate the existence of adjacent habitats that were not included within the sanctuary boundaries but are likely important in maintaining the integrity of the sanctuary ecosystem. One such situation occurs at Stetson Bank, where a portion of the topographic feature was not included within the original boundary. Areas such as these should be considered for inclusion within the sanctuary. Furthermore, it is becoming evident that we need to view the reefs and banks of the northwestern Gulf of Mexico as an interconnected network of biological communities. It is apparent from past studies on certain species, such as sea turtles (Hickerson 2000), and recent observations of fish moving between banks in deep habitats that certain animals use resources on more than one

bank during their lifetimes. The sanctuary staff is therefore expanding its programs to investigate the movement of animals among the banks, initially focusing on mantas and whale sharks.

During public scoping meetings that are part of the sanctuary management plan review process, numerous comments were received from individuals, organizations and agencies indicating support for boundary expansion. A boundary expansion working group was formed by the Sanctuary Advisory Council and a boundary expansion workshop was held. Invited experts, members of the Sanctuary Advisory Council and the public participated. The working group evaluated and ranked 17 banks and associated topographic features, and seven alternatives for boundary expansion were developed and presented to the Sanctuary Advisory Council. The council submitted its recommendation to modify the boundaries for Stetson Bank and East and West Flower Garden Banks. The alternative also included the creation of a sanctuary boundary around Horseshoe Bank, an area between East and West Flower Garden Banks (Figure 23). It also recommended boundaries to include the following areas: MacNeil, Rankin, 28 Fathom, Bright, Geyer, Sonnier, McGrail, and Alderdice Banks.

Harvesting

To minimize the impacts of harvesting, current regulations limit fishing in the sanctuary to conventional hook-and-line methods. In spite of the restrictions on most types of fishing gear and the remote location of the sanctuary, there is concern that unanticipated fishing impacts are occurring at the Flower Garden Banks. During the public scoping process for management plan review conducted in October 2006, fishing was identified as a primary issue of concern. Many commented that sanctuary management should consider the use of no-take marine reserves within all or part of the area. The Sanctuary Advisory Council has also identified fishing impacts as a priority issue and created a subcommittee to explore management strategies to address the concerns. The Advisory Council has developed both fishing and visitor use working groups. A fishing impacts workshop was attended by experts, advisory council members, and the public. These groups have recommended that sanctuary management proceed with an eight-year experimental closure to measure the effects of fishing and diving on the resources of the sanctuary. The experimental design of this closure was discussed during meetings in April 2008.

Enforcement and surveillance are difficult within the sanctuary due to the distance from shore. Sanctuary staff relies heavily on assistance from the U.S. Coast Guard and NOAA Fisheries for enforcement. Although both agencies have been very cooperative in the past, there is little enforcement within the sanctuary at this time. This will change in the near future, as a dedicated sanctuary vessel was delivered in June 2008 (Figure 24). This vessel will provide the ability to elevate the level of sanctuary surveillance and monitoring on site. Further, the Flower Garden Banks National Marine Sanctuary will collaborate with NOAA Enforcement and the Coast Guard to carry representatives on board and conduct enforcement actions as necessary.

In response to the results of high levels of mercury and ciguatera, sanctuary management has issued a request for samples from fishermen targeting winter populations of grouper and wahoo in the sanctuary. Sanctuary staff will collaborate with NOAA's National Centers for Coastal Ocean Science, NOAA's Southeast Fisheries Science Center, the University of Texas Marine Science Institute, and the U.S. Food and Drug Administration to analyze the samples. The level and longevity of this investigation will depend on the availability of funds: however, sanctuary management is committed to providing vessel time and resources to obtain samples on at least a quarterly basis.

Sanctuary staff also engages in outreach efforts to reach harvesting communities and inform users of sanctuary resources and regulations. Current outreach to this community is achieved by providing information on the sanctuary Web site, occasional one-on-one encounters with fishermen in the sanctuary, and a summary of fishing regulations distributed through outreach staff and NOAA Fisheries fishery reporting specialists (port agents). The Flower Garden Banks National Marine Sanctuary Advisory Council includes designated seats for representatives of both the recreational and commercial fishing constituent groups.

Invasive Species

Sanctuary management supports long-term monitoring of the coral reef area of the sanctuary to examine the health of the ecosystem and to detect the appearance of invasive species. This regular monitoring provides the site with advance warning and the opportunity to take immediate steps to address invasive species issues. Invertebrate monitoring at East and West Flower Garden Banks is conducted primarily by contractors for the long-term benthic monitoring program, supported by NOAA and the Minerals Management Service. Sanctuary staff conduct monitoring of benthic communities at Stetson Bank. Fish monitoring is conducted through the long-term monitoring program as well as by volunteers associated with the Reef Environmental Education Foundation (REEF) and scientists from NOAA's National Centers for Coastal Ocean Science (NCCOS). The policy related to exotic or invasive species within the Flower Garden Banks National Marine Sanctuary is to remove them—if possible—as soon as they are encountered. Removal can only be undertaken by properly permitted entities.

Oil and Gas Infrastructure

Direct consultation is conducted with the Minerals Management Service regarding any proposed oil and gas development within a four mile buffer area around the banks of the sanctuary. In this way, concerns of sanctuary management are incorporated in the review of those proposals so that specific resource protection issues can be addressed. In addition, sanctuary regulations prohibit discharging pollutants in the sanctuary and disturbing the seafloor. Within the sanctuary oil and gas exploration and development is not allowed in areas designated by the MMS as "no-activity zones."

The sanctuary staff also conducts training and information sharing activities to maintain collaborative relationships with the oil and gas industry. These include shared research and learning activities and one-on-one interactions with industry personnel and presentations at training sessions sponsored by industry for their offshore operations personnel. Such activities allow industry personnel the opportunity to learn about the sanctuary and the resources they are helping to protect when they comply with the highest operating standards. Sanctuary staff also participates in spill drills with the industry and MMS and works with regional response teams on contingency plans for spills and dispersant use policies.

Pollutant Discharges

The discharge of most pollutants and other material is prohibited by current sanctuary regulations. However, there are exceptions included in the regulations for "biodegradable effluents incidental to vessel use and generated by marine sanitation devices" approved by the U.S. Coast Guard, "graywater" (water from deck wash-down, showers and sinks) and engine exhaust. However, as previously noted, effluents discharged by approved marine sanitation devices can still contain a variety of pollutants, including high levels of nutrients and other contaminants. In addition, graywater may also contain harmful material, including detergents and bleach that are known to be toxic to corals. Further restrictions on the discharge of pollutants could be considered by the sanctuary, including the designation of the area as a "no discharge zone."

Shipping and Transport

Historically, significant impacts on corals resulted from anchoring of large ocean-going vessels at the Flower Garden Banks. One anchoring incident can destroy hundreds of years of reef growth within minutes. This impact was minimized by the designation of the sanctuary in 1992, which prohibited anchoring with minor exceptions. In 2001, the sanctuary regulations were changed to prohibit all anchoring within the sanctuary. In addition, the sanctuary has been designated as a "no-anchor" area by the International Maritime Organization (IMO) so that the restriction appears on international charts most commonly used by foreign-flagged vessels. The designation of the Flower Garden Banks National Marine Sanctuary as a no-anchor zone by the IMO was the first time in history that this action had been taken for the purpose of habitat protection. This no-anchor regulation is further strengthened through the NOAA Fisheries designation of the banks within the sanctuary as Habitat Areas of Particular Concern, protecting coral reefs by prohibiting anchoring by fishing vessels.

Visitor Use

Recreational divers constitute the largest user group within the sanctuary. To address potential impacts from this group, sanctuary staff frequently engages in outreach to divers through participation in dive-related trade shows, interactions with dive clubs, and interpretive programs. One such effort is the "Naturalist on Board" program aimed at recreational divers visiting the sanctuary aboard commercial dive charter vessels. Trained volunteer interpreters join commercial dive expeditions to convey educational messages and raise awareness of and appreciation for sanctuary resources.

Another potential impact from visitors, especially those arriving on private vessels, is that caused by anchoring. Mooring buoys have

been installed at prominent dive locations at the Flower Garden Banks to allow visitors to use the sanctuary without damaging its resources. In the future, consideration will have to be given to the number and placement of mooring buoys and management of the mooring buoy system. The 17 buoys currently in place in the sanctuary concentrate use in certain locations. As usage levels increase it may be necessary to disperse use by adding new buoys and temporarily removing others to limit inputs and allow damaged areas to recover. Also, regulations are in place that prohibit taking or injuring coral or coral reef organisms, preventing divers from collecting coral or other organisms.

Wildlife Interactions

Divers are drawn to the Flower Garden Banks for the opportunity to observe a variety of large marine animals, including sea turtles, manta rays and whale sharks. Often, divers are able to approach these animals at very close range, sometimes so close that the animals can be touched or in some cases held onto for a "ride." Many times, the animals do not react negatively to such activities, giving the impression that these actions are innocuous. However, touching, chasing or otherwise harassing these animals may alter their behavior and have other detrimental impacts. Sea turtles are protected from these activities through the Endangered Species Act. Sanctuary management may consider providing similar protection to rays, sharks and other large animals.

Hurricanes

Hurricanes are a natural phenomenon that cannot be controlled or addressed directly by management actions. As with coral bleaching, the primary way to address the impacts of hurricane damage is to attempt to manage, as much as possible, the other stressors over which we do have some control. Coral reefs have existed with hurricanes for eons, and although reefs may experience severe damage from hurricanes, given enough time and good environmental conditions, the reefs will recover. However, reefs are under assault from a variety of other factors, and if they are also subjected to pollution, sedimentation and ecosystem manipulation, they will not recover as quickly as in the past. Knowledge of the dynamics of the ecology of coral reefs will aid in management of these systems that are subjected to natural impacts such as hurricanes.

Concluding Remarks

The natural resources of Flower Garden Banks National Marine Sanctuary are in generally good condition. When the coral reefs of the Flower Garden Banks are compared to other reefs of the western Atlantic and Caribbean, they continue to surpass most in terms of coral cover, health and ecosystem conditions. Coral diversity, though lower in comparison to most Caribbean reefs, remains stable at these high-latitude banks (and may even be increasing). Recent events and observations, however, have identified potential warning signals, and suggest that the banks are not as isolated from threats as in the past. In the last few years, sanctuary staff, independent scientists, and frequent visitors to the banks have documented coral disease and coral bleaching events, the appearance of potentially invasive species, and evidence of a decline in the number and size of some prominent fish species, which could have cascading impacts on the bank ecosystem. Current regulations and enforcement capabilities may not be adequate to address the sources of some of these impacts. Further, recent human health problems stemming from ciguatera poisoning incidents, as well as evidence of mercury contamination in some fish species, will require enhanced research, monitoring, and management in these areas.

In this era of significant decline of coral reefs throughout the world, resilience is key to the survival of this critical ecosystem. It has been estimated that coral cover on reefs in the Caribbean has declined by an average of 80% in the last three decades (Gardner et al. 2003). It is generally agreed that these declines are not due to a single cause, but have resulted from multiple stressors acting together to alter ecosystem conditions and resulting in widespread deterioration. Some stressors (large-scale ocean warming, hurricanes, etc.) cannot be controlled by resource managers, but others (many of those associated with human uses) can be addressed through proper management. Coral reefs that have remained in good health during this period, such as those within the Flower Garden Banks National Marine Sanctuary, may provide important insight in understanding resilience and other factors that sustain coral reef vitality. Therefore, it is more important than ever to protect remaining healthy reefs from impacts that can be addressed through management actions, both for their own sake and in order to help us promote the recovery of other coral reefs.

Photo All American Marine Inc.

Figure 24. The new Flower Garden Banks National Marine Sanctuary research vessel, the R/V *Manta*, was dedicated in Galveston on June 27, 2008. This 83 ft. catamaran will greatly enhance research, education and outreach, response and enforcement.

Acknowledgements

Flower Garden Banks National Marine Sanctuary would like to acknowledge the assistance of Jennifer DeBose (Flower Garden Banks National Marine Sanctuary) and Sarah Fangman (Office of National Marine Sanctuaries: Southeast Atlantic, Gulf of Mexico, and Caribbean Region) who were instrumental in developing and reviewing this document. We would also like to thank staff from NOAA's Southeast Fisheries Science Center for reviewing a draft of this report. Finally, we also wish to thank Dr. Rich Aronson (Dauphin Island Sea Lab), Dr. Thomas Bright, Mr. Gregory Boland (Minerals Management Service), and Dr. Judy Lang for their helpful review and comments on this document.

Cited Resources

Allison, W.R. 2005. Snorkeler damage to reef corals in the Maldive Islands. Coral Reefs 15(4):215-218.

Aronson, R.B., W.F. Precht, T.J.T. Murdoch and M.L. Robbart. 2005. Long-Term persistence of coral assemblages on the Flower Garden Banks, northwestern Gulf of Mexico: Implications for science and management. Dedicated Issue, Flower Garden Banks National Marine Sanctuary, Gulf of Mexico Science 25(1):84-94.

Baggett, L.S. 1985. Patterns of coral recruitment at the East Flower Garden bank. M.S. Thesis, Texas A&M University, College Station, Texas. 55 pp.

Bernhardt, S. P. 2000. Photographic Monitoring of Benthic Biota at Stetson Bank. M.S. Thesis. Texas A&M University, College Station, Texas.

Bright, T.J. and L.H. Pequegnat (eds.) 1974. Biota of the West Flower Garden Bank. Gulf Publishing Company, Book Division, Houston, Texas. 435 pp.

Bright, T.J., G.P. Kraemer, G.A. Minnery and S.T. Viada. 1984. Hermatypes of the Flower Garden Banks. Bulletin of Marine Science 34 (3), 461-476.

Bright, T.J., S.R. Gittings and R. Zingula. 1991. Occurrence of Atlantic reef corals on offshore platforms in the northwestern Gulf of Mexico. NE Gulf Science 12(1):55-60.

Bruno, J.F., L.E. Petes, C.D. Harvell, and A. Hettinger. 2003. Nutrient enrichment can increase the severity of coral diseases. Ecology Letters 6:1056-1061.

Childs, Jeffery N. 2001. The Occurrence, habitat use and behavior of sharks and rays associating with topographic highs in the Gulf of Mexico. M.S. Thesis. Texas A&M University, College Station, Texas.

Coleman, F.C., W.F. Figueira, J.S. Ueland and L.B. Crowder. 2004. The impact of United States recreational fisheries on marine fish populations. Science 305:1958-1960.

Continental Shelf Assoc., Inc. 1996. Long-term monitoring at the East and West Flower Garden Banks. OCS Study MMS 96-0046. U.S. Department of the Interior, Minerals Management Service, Gulf of Mexico OCS Region, New Orleans, Louisiana. 77 pp. + app.

Deslarzes, K.J.P. and A. Lugo-Fernández. 2007. Influence of terrigenous runoff on offshore coral reefs: An example from the Flower Garden Banks, Gulf of Mexico. Pages 126-160 in Aronson, R.B., ed. Geological approaches to coral reef ecology. Springer, New York, New York.

Dokken, Q.R., I.R. MacDonald, J.W. Tunnell, Jr., C.R. Beaver, G.S. Boland, and D.K. Hagman. 1999. Long-term monitoring at the East and West Flower Garden Banks, 1996-1997. U.S. Department of the Interior, Minerals Management Service, Gulf of Mexico OCS Region, New Orleans, Louisiana. OCS Study MMS99-0005.

Dokken, Q.R., I.R. MacDonald, J.W. Tunnell, Jr., T. Wade, K. Withers, S.J. Dilworth, T.W. Bates, C.R. Beaver, and C.M.Rigaud. 2003. Long-term monitoring at the East and West Flower Garden Banks, 1998-2001: Final Report. U.S. Department of the Interior, Minerals Management Service, Gulf of Mexico OCS Region, New Orleans, Louisiana. OCS Study MMS 2003-031. 90 pp.

Engas, A., Lokkeborg, S., Ona, E. and Soldal, A.V. 1996. Effects of seismic shooting on local abundance and catch rates of cod (Gadus morhua) and haddock (Melanogrammus aeglefinus). Canadian Journal of Fisheries and Aquatic Sciences 53: 2238-2249.

Fenner, D. and K. Banks. 2004. Orange cup coral Tubastraea coccinea invades Florida and the Flower Garden Banks, Northwestern Gulf of Mexico. Coral Reefs 23:505-507.

Gardner, J. V., L.A. Mayer, J.E. Hughes Clarke and A. Kleiner. 1998. High-resolution multibeam bathymetry of East and West Flower Gardens and Stetson Banks, Gulf of Mexico. Gulf of Mexico Science XVI No. 2:128.

Gardner, T.A., I.M. Côté, J.A. Gill, A. Grant and A.R. Watkinson. 2003. Long-term region-wide declines in Caribbean corals. Science 301: 958-960.

Gittings, S.R. 1985. Notes on barnacles (Cirripedia: Thoracica) from the Gulf of Mexico. Gulf Research Reports 8(1):35-41.

Gittings, S.R. 1998. Reef community stability on the Flower Garden Banks, Northwest Gulf of Mexico. Gulf of Mexico Science XVI No. 2:161.

Gittings, S.R. and G.S. Boland. 1991. Long-term monitoring on the Flower Garden Banks: study design and field methods. pp. 24-28 In: Proc.: Eleventh Ann. Gulf of Mexico Information Transfer Meeting. U.S. Deptartment of the Interior, Minerals Management Service, New Orleans, Louisiana. Contract No. 14-35-0001-30499. OCS Study MMS-91-0040. 524 pp.

Gittings, S.R., T.J. Bright, W.W. Schroeder, W.W. Sager, R. Rezak, and J.S. Laswell. 1992a. Biotic assemblages and ecological controls on topographic features in the northeast Gulf of Mexico. Bulletin of Marine Science 50(3):435-455.

Gittings, S.R., G.S. Boland, K.J.P. Deslarzes, D.K. Hagman and B.S. Holland. 1992b. Long-term monitoring at the East and West Flower Garden Banks. Final Rept. OCS Study/MMS 92-006. U.S. Department of the Interior, Minerals Management Service, Gulf of Mexico OCS Regional Office, New Orleans, Louisiana. 206 pp.

Gittings, S.R., K.J.P. Deslarzes, D.K. Hagman, and G.S. Boland. 1992c. Reef coral populations and growth on the Flower Garden Banks, northwest Gulf of Mexico. Proc. 7th Int. Coral Reef Symposium 1:90-96.

Gittings, S.R., C.L. Ostrom, and K.J.P. Deslarzes. 1997. Regulation by reason: Science and management in the Flower Gardens Sanctuary, northwest Gulf of Mexico. Proc. 8th Int. Coral Reef Symposium 2:1967-1972.

Gold, J.R., C.P. Burridge and T.F. Turner. 2004. A modified stepping-stone model of population structure in red drum, Sciaenops ocellatus (Sciaenidae), from the northern Gulf of Mexico. Genetica 111 305-317.

Hagman, D.K. 2001. Reproductive dynamics of coral reef biota at the Flower Gardens. Ph.D. Dissertation, University of Texas at Austin, Austin, Texas.

Hagman, D.K. and S.R. Gittings. 1992. Coral bleaching on high latitude reefs at the Flower Garden Banks, NW Gulf of Mexico. Proc. 7th Int. Coral Reef Symposium 1:38-43.

Hawkins, J.P., C.M. Roberts, T. Van't Hof, K. de Meyer, J. Tratalos, Aldam. 1999. Effects of recreational scuba diving on Caribbean coral and fish communities. Conservation Biology 13, 888-897.

Hickerson, E. L. 2000. Assessing and tracking resident, immature loggerheads (Caretta caretta) in and around the Flower Garden Banks, northwest Gulf of Mexico. M.S. Thesis. Texas A&M University, College Station, Texas. 102 pp.

Hickerson, E.L. and G.P. Schmahl. 2005. Status of the coral reef ecosystems of the Flower Garden Banks, Stetson Bank, and other banks in the Northwestern Gulf of Mexico. Pp. 201-221 In: The state of coral reef ecosystems of the United States and Pacific Freely Associated States. NOAA/NCCOS. 522 pp.

Kennicutt, M.C., J.M. Brooks, S. Carr, R. Darnell, R.E. Fay, R.H. Green, D. Harper, J. McEachran, P. Montagna, B.J. Presley, R. Rezak, S. Safe, J.W. Fournie, S.J. McDonald, D.A.. Wiesenburg, F.J. Kelly, T. Wade, and G.A. Wolff. 1995. Gulf of Mexico Offshore Monitoring Experiment (GOOMEX) Phase I: Sublethal response to contaminant exposure. Final Report. Technical Summary: MMS Publication 95-0045.

Kraemer, G.P. 1982. Population levels and growth rates of the scleractinian corals within the Diploria-Montastrea-Porites zones of the East and West Flower Garden banks. M.S. Thesis, Texas A&M University, College Station, Texas. 138 pp.

Lang, J.C., Deslarzes, K.J.P., Schmahl, G.P. 2001. The Flower Garden Banks: remarkable reefs in the NW Gulf of Mexico. Coral Reefs 20:126.

Lugo-Fernandez, A. 1998. Ecological implications of hydrography and circulation to the Flower Garden Banks, northwest Gulf of Mexico. Gulf of Mexico Science 16(2):144-160.

Lugo-Fernandez, A., K.J.P. Deslarzes, J.M. Price, G.S. Boland and M.V. Morin. 2001. Inferring probable dispersal of Flower Garden Banks Coral Larvae (Gulf of Mexico) using observed and simulated drifter trajectories. Continental Shelf Research 21:47-67.

Marano-Briggs, K. 2006. Does dive equipment spread coral and human disease? 106th General Meeting of the American Society for Microbiology. Session 265/N, Paper N-164. http://www.asm.org/Media/index.asp?bid=42940.

Marshall, P.A. and H.Z. Schuttenberg. 2006. A reef manager's guide to coral bleaching. Great Barrier Reef Marine Park Authority, Australia (ISBN 1-876945-40-0).

National Marine Sanctuary Program. 2004. A monitoring framework for the National Marine Sanctuary System. U.S. Department of Commerce, National Oceanic and Atmospheric Administration, National Ocean Service. Silver Spring, Maryland. 22 pp.

Orr, J.C. and 25 other authors. 2005. Anthropogenic ocean acidification over the twenty-first century and its impacts on calcifying organisms. Nature 437:681-686.

Pattengill, C.V. 1998. The Structure and Persistence of Reef Fish Assemblages of the Flower Garden Banks National Marine Sanctuary. Ph. D. Dissertation. Texas A&M University, College Station, Texas. 164 pp.

Pattengill-Semmens, C.V. 1999. Occurrence of a unique color morph in the smooth trunkfish (Lactophrys triqueter L.) at the Flower Garden Banks and Stetson Bank, Northwest Gulf of Mexico. Bulletin of Marine Science 65(2):587-591.

Pattengill-Semmens, C.V. and S. R. Gittings. 2003. A rapid assessment of the Flower Garden Banks National Marine Sanctuary (stony corals, algae and fishes). pp. 500-511 In: Status of Coral Reefs in the Western Atlantic: Results of Initial Surveys, Atlantic and Gulf Rapid Reef Assessment (AGRRA) Program. E. Judith C. Lang.

Pearson, W.H., Skalski, J.R. and Malme, C.I. 1992. Effects of sounds from a geophysical survey device on behavior of captive rockfish (Sebastes spp.). Canadian Journal of Fisheries and Aquatic Sciences 49: 1343-1356.

Precht, W.F., M. L. Robbart, G.S. Boland and G.P. Schmahl. 2005. Establishment and initial analysis of deep reef stations (32-40m) at the East Flower Garden Bank. Dedicated Issue, Flower Garden Banks National Marine Sanctuary, Gulf of Mexico Science 25(1):124-127.

Precht W.F., R.B. Aronson, K.J.P. Deslarzes, M.L. Robbart, T.J.T. Murdoch, A. Gelber, D. Evans, B. Gearheart and B. Zimmer. (in press) Long-term monitoring at the East and West Flower Garden Banks, 2004-2005; Final report. U.S. Department of the Interior, Minerals Management Service, Gulf of Mexico OCS Region, New Orleans, Louisiana. OCS Study MMS.

Rezak, R., T.J. Bright, and D.W. McGrail. 1985. Reefs and Banks of the Northwestern Gulf of Mexico: Their Geological, Biological, and Physical Dynamics. John Wiley and Sons, New York, New York. 259 pp.

Rexing, S.R. 2004. Structure and trophic importance of benthic macroinfaunal communities around live-bottom reefs at Flower Garden Banks National Marine Sanctuary. M.S. Thesis. College of Charleston, Charleston, South Carolina.

Robbart, M.L., R.B. Aronson, L. Duncan, and B. Zimmer. In press. Post-hurricane assessment of sensitive habitats of the Flower Garden Banks Vicinity. U.S. Department of the Interior, Minerals Management Service, Gulf of Mexico OCS Region, New Orleans, Louisiana. OCS Study MMS.

Sammarco P.W., Atchison A.D. and Boland G.S. 2004 Expansion of coral communities within the Northern Gulf of Mexico via offshore oil and gas platforms. Marine Ecology Progress Series 280:129-143.

Schmahl, G.P. 2002. Status of the Flower Garden Banks of the Northwestern Gulf of Mexico. Pp. 143-150 In: The State of Coral Reef Ecosystems of the United States and Pacific Freely Associated States: 2002. Turgeon et al. NOAA/NCCOS.

Schmahl, G.P. and Emma Hickerson. 2004. Pp. 431-448 In: Status of Coral Reefs in the U.S. Caribbean and Gulf of Mexico: Florida, Flower Garden Banks, Puerto Rico, U.S. Virgin Islands, Navassa. In Status of Coral Reefs of the World: 2004. Ed. Clive Wilkinson.

Snell, T.L., D.W. Foltz and P.W. Sammarco. 1998. Variation in Morphology vs. Conservation of a Mitochondrial Gene in Montastraea cavernosa (Cnidaria, Scleractinia). Gulf of Mexico Science XVI No. 2:188.

Taylor, D.D. 1973. The distribution of heavy metals in reef-dwelling groupers (Serranidae) in the Gulf of Mexico and Caribbean Sea. Ph.D. Dissertation, Texas A&M University, College Station, Texas. 250 pp.

Villareal, T.A., S. Hanson, S. Qualia, E.L.E. Jester, H.R. Granade, R.W. Dickey. 2007. Petroleum Production Platforms as sites for the expansion of ciguatera in the northwestern Gulf of Mexico. Harmful Algae 6 (2007) 253-259.

Waddell, J.E. and A.M. Clarke (eds.), 2008. The State of Coral Reef Ecosystems of the United States and Pacific Freely Associated States: 2008. NOAA Technical Memorandum NOS NCCOS 73. NOAA/NCCOS Center for Coastal Monitoring and Assessment's Biogeography Team. Silver Spring, Maryland. 569 pp.

Weaver, D.C. and L.A. Rocha. 2007. A new species of Halichoeres (Teleostei Labridae) from the Western Gulf of Mexico. Copeia 2007 4:798-807.

Zimmer, B., W. Precht, E. Hickerson and J. Sinclair. 2006. Discovery of Acropora palmata at the Flower Garden Banks National Marine Sanctuary, northwestern Gulf of Mexico. Coral Reefs. Department of the Interior. 10.1007/s00338-005-0054-9.

Additional Resources

Flower Garden Banks National Marine Sanctuary: http://flowergarden.noaa.gov

Louisiana Department of Wildlife and Fisheries: http://www.wlf.louisiana.gov

Louisiana Department of Wildlife and Fisheries Artificial Reef Program: http://www.wlf.louisiana.gov/licenses/permits/artificialreefprogram

Marine Protected Areas of the United States: http://www.mpa.gov

Minerals Management Service: http://www.mms.gov

Minerals Management Service Web site, Gulf of Mexico Maps and Spatial Data: http://www.gomr.mms.gov/homepg/pubinfo/mapsandspatial-data.html

National Oceanic and Atmospheric Administration: http://www.noaa.gov

News @ Nature Web site, Divers carry pathogens in their wetsuits: http://www.nature.com/news/2006/060522/full/060522-14.html

NOAA's National Centers for Coastal Ocean Science: http://coastalscience.noaa.gov

NOAA's National Marine Fisheries Service: http://www.nmfs.noaa.gov

NOAA's National Marine Fisheries Service Southeast Regional Office: http://sero.nmfs.noaa.gov

NOAA's National Marine Fisheries Service Web site, Gulf of Mexico Red Snapper Information and Programs: http://sero.nmfs.noaa.gov/sf/RedSnapper/RedSnapperDocs.htm

NOAA's Office of National Marine Sanctuaries: http://sanctuaries.noaa.gov

NOAA's Southeast Fisheries Science Center: http://www.sefsc.noaa.gov/

Reef Environmental Education Foundation: http://www.reef.org

Texas Parks and Wildlife: http://www.tpwd.state.tx.us

Texas Parks and Wildlife Artificial Reef Program: http://www.tpwd.state.tx.us/landwater/water/habitats/artificial_reef

U.S. Geological Survey: http://www.usgs.gov

U.S. Food and Drug Administration: http://www.fda.gov

University of Texas Marine Science Institute: http://www.utmsi.utexas.edu

Appendix: Rating Scale for System-Wide Monitoring Questions

The purpose of this appendix is to clarify the 17 questions and possible responses used to report the condition of sanctuary resources in "Condition Reports" for all national marine sanctuaries. Individual staff and partners utilized this guidance, as well as their own informed and detailed understanding of the site to make judgments about the status and trends of sanctuary resources.

The questions derive from the Office of National Marine Sanctuaries' mission, and a system-wide monitoring framework (National Marine Sanctuary Program 2004) developed to ensure the timely flow of data and information to those responsible for managing and protecting resources in the ocean and coastal zone, and to those that use, depend on and study the ecosystems encompassed by the sanctuaries. They are being used to guide staff and partners at each of the 14 sites in the sanctuary system in the development of this first periodic sanctuary condition report. The questions are meant to set the limits of judgments so that responses can be confined to certain reporting categories that will later be compared among all sites and combined. Evaluations of status and trends may be based on interpretation of quantitative and, when necessary, non-quantitative assessments and observations of scientists, managers and users.

Following a brief discussion about each question, statements are presented that were used to judge the status and assign a corresponding color code. These statements are customized for each question. In addition, the following options are available for all questions: "N/A" — the question does not apply; and "Undet." — resource status is undetermined.

Symbols used to indicate trends are the same for all questions: "▲" - conditions appear to be improving; "—" - conditions do not appear to be changing; "▼" - conditions appear to be declining; and "?" - trend is undetermined.

Water Stressors

1. | **Are specific or multiple stressors, including changing oceanographic and atmospheric conditions, affecting water quality and how are they changing?**

This is meant to capture shifts in conditions arising from certain changing physical processes and anthropogenic inputs. Factors resulting in regionally accelerated rates of change in water temperature, salinity, dissolved oxygen or water clarity could all be judged to reduce water quality. Localized changes in circulation or sedimentation resulting, for example, from coastal construction or dredge spoil disposal, can affect light penetration, salinity regimes, oxygen levels, productivity, waste transport and other factors that influence habitat and living resource quality. Human inputs, generally in the form of contaminants from point or non-point sources, including fertilizers, pesticides, hydrocarbons, heavy metals and sewage, are common causes of environmental degradation, often in combination rather than alone. Certain biotoxins, such as domoic acid, may be of particular interest to specific sanctuaries. When present in the water column, any of these contaminants can affect marine life by direct contact or ingestion, or through bioaccumulation via the food chain.

[Note: Over time, accumulation in sediments can sequester and concentrate contaminants. Their effects may manifest only when the sediments are resuspended during storm or other energetic events. In such cases, reports of status should be made under Question 7 – Habitat contaminants.]

Good	Conditions do not appear to have the potential to negatively affect living resources or habitat quality.
Good/Fair	Selected conditions may preclude full development of living resource assemblages and habitats, but are not likely to cause substantial or persistent declines.
Fair	Selected conditions may inhibit the development of assemblages and may cause measurable but not severe declines in living resources and habitats.
Fair/Poor	Selected conditions have caused or are likely to cause severe declines in some but not all living resources and habitats.
Poor	Selected conditions have caused or are likely to cause severe declines in most if not all living resources and habitats.

Water
Eutrophic
Condition

2. | **What is the eutrophic condition of sanctuary waters and how is it changing?**

Nutrient enrichment often leads to planktonic and/or benthic algae blooms. Some affect benthic communities directly through space competition. Overgrowth and other competitive interactions (e.g., accumulation of algal-sediment mats) often lead to shifts in dominance in the benthic assemblage. Disease incidence and frequency can also be affected by algae competition and the resulting chemistry along competitive boundaries. Blooms can also affect water column conditions, including light penetration and plankton availability, which can alter pelagic food webs. Harmful algal blooms often affect resources, as biotoxins are released into the water and air, and oxygen can be depleted.

Good   Conditions do not appear to have the potential to negatively affect living resources or habitat quality.

Good/Fair   Selected conditions may preclude full development of living resource assemblages and habitats, but are not likely to cause substantial or persistent declines.

Fair   Selected conditions may inhibit the development of assemblages and may cause measurable but not severe declines in living resources and habitats.

Fair/Poor   Selected conditions have caused or are likely to cause severe declines in some but not all living resources and habitats.

Poor   Selected conditions have caused or are likely to cause severe declines in most if not all living resources and habitats.

Water
Human Health

3. | **Do sanctuary waters pose risks to human health and how are they changing?**

Human health concerns are generally aroused by evidence of contamination (usually bacterial or chemical) in bathing waters or fish intended for consumption. They also emerge when harmful algal blooms are reported or when cases of respiratory distress or other disorders attributable to harmful algal blooms increase dramatically. Any of these conditions should be considered in the course of judging the risk to humans posed by waters in a marine sanctuary.

Some sites may have access to specific information on beach and shellfish conditions. In particular, beaches may be closed when criteria for safe water body contact are exceeded, or shellfish harvesting may be prohibited when contaminant loads or infection rates exceed certain levels. These conditions can be evaluated in the context of the descriptions below.

Good   Conditions do not appear to have the potential to negatively affect human health.

Good/Fair   Selected conditions that have the potential to affect human health may exist but human impacts have not been reported.

Fair   Selected conditions have resulted in isolated human impacts, but evidence does not justify widespread or persistent concern.

Fair/Poor   Selected conditions have caused or are likely to cause severe impacts, but cases to date have not suggested a pervasive problem.

Poor   Selected conditions warrant widespread concern and action, as large-scale, persistent and/or repeated severe impacts are likely or have occurred.

Water
Human Activities

4. | **What are the levels of human activities that may influence water quality and how are they changing?**

Among the human activities in or near sanctuaries that affect water quality are those involving direct discharges (transiting vessels, visiting vessels, onshore and offshore industrial facilities, public wastewater facilities), those that contribute contaminants to stream, river, and water control discharges (agriculture, runoff from impermeable surfaces through storm drains, conversion of land use), and those releasing airborne chemicals that subsequently deposit via particulates at sea (vessels, land-based traffic, power plants, manufacturing facilities, refineries). In addition, dredging and trawling can cause resuspension of contaminants in sediments.

Good	Few or no activities occur that are likely to negatively affect water quality.
Good/Fair	Some potentially harmful activities exist, but they do not appear to have had a negative effect on water quality.
Fair	Selected activities have resulted in measurable resource impacts, but evidence suggests effects are localized, not widespread.
Fair/Poor	Selected activities have caused or are likely to cause severe impacts, and cases to date suggest a pervasive problem.
Poor	Selected activities warrant widespread concern and action, as large-scale, persistent and/or repeated severe impacts have occurred or are likely to occur.

Habitat
Abundance & Distribution

5. | **What are the abundance and distribution of major habitat types and how are they changing?**

Habitat loss is of paramount concern when it comes to protecting marine and terrestrial ecosystems. Of greatest concern to sanctuaries are changes caused, either directly or indirectly, by human activities. The loss of shoreline is recognized as a problem indirectly caused by human activities. Habitats with submerged aquatic vegetation are often altered by changes in water conditions in estuaries, bays, and nearshore waters. Intertidal zones can be affected for long periods by spills or by chronic pollutant exposure. Beaches and haul-out areas can be littered with dangerous marine debris, as can the water column or benthic habitats. Sandy subtidal areas and hardbottoms are frequently disturbed or destroyed by trawling. Even rocky areas several hundred meters deep are increasingly affected by certain types of trawls, bottom longlines and fish traps. Groundings, anchors and divers damage submerged reefs. Cables and pipelines disturb corridors across numerous habitat types and can be destructive if they become mobile. Shellfish dredging removes, alters and fragments habitats.

The result of these activities is the gradual reduction of the extent and quality of marine habitats. Losses can often be quantified through visual surveys and to some extent using high-resolution mapping. This question asks about the quality of habitats compared to those that would be expected without human impacts. The status depends on comparison to a baseline that existed in the past — one toward which restoration efforts might aim.

Good	Habitats are in pristine or near-pristine condition and are unlikely to preclude full community development.
Good/Fair	Selected habitat loss or alteration has taken place, precluding full development of living resource assemblages, but it is unlikely to cause substantial or persistent degradation in living resources or water quality.
Fair	Selected habitat loss or alteration may inhibit the development of assemblages, and may cause measurable but not severe declines in living resources or water quality.
Fair/Poor	Selected habitat loss or alteration has caused or is likely to cause severe declines in some but not all living resources or water quality.
Poor	Selected habitat loss or alteration has caused or is likely to cause severe declines in most if not all living resources or water quality.

Habitat Structure

6. | **What is the condition of biologically structured habitats and how is it changing?**

Many organisms depend on the integrity of their habitats and that integrity is largely determined by the condition of particular living organisms. Coral reefs may be the best known examples of such biologically-structured habitats. Not only is the substrate itself biogenic, but the diverse assemblages residing within and on the reefs depend on and interact with each other in tightly linked food webs. They also depend on each other for the recycling of wastes, hygiene and the maintenance of water quality, among other requirements.

Kelp beds may not be biogenic habitats to the extent of coral reefs, but kelp provides essential habitat for assemblages that would not reside or function together without it. There are other communities of organisms that are also similarly co-dependent, such as hard-bottom communities, which may be structured by bivalves, octocorals, coralline algae or other groups that generate essential habitat for other species. Intertidal assemblages structured by mussels, barnacles and algae are another example, seagrass beds another. This question is intended to address these types of places where organisms form structures (habitats) on which other organisms depend.

Good	Habitats are in pristine or near-pristine condition and are unlikely to preclude full community development.
Good/Fair	Selected habitat loss or alteration has taken place, precluding full development of living resources, but it is unlikely to cause substantial or persistent degradation in living resources or water quality.
Fair	Selected habitat loss or alteration may inhibit the development of living resources and may cause measurable but not severe declines in living resources or water quality.
Fair/Poor	Selected habitat loss or alteration has caused or is likely to cause severe declines in some but not all living resources or water quality.
Poor	Selected habitat loss or alteration has caused or is likely to cause severe declines in most if not all living resources or water quality.

Habitat Contaminants

7. | **What are the contaminant concentrations in sanctuary habitats and how are they changing?**

This question addresses the need to understand the risk posed by contaminants within benthic formations, such as soft sediments, hard bottoms, or biogenic organisms. In the first two cases, the contaminants can become available when released via disturbance. They can also pass upwards through the food chain after being ingested by bottom dwelling prey species. The contaminants of concern generally include pesticides, hydrocarbons and heavy metals, but the specific concerns of individual sanctuaries may differ substantially.

Good	Contaminants do not appear to have the potential to negatively affect living resources or water quality.
Good/Fair	Selected contaminants may preclude full development of living resource assemblages, but are not likely to cause substantial or persistent degradation.
Fair	Selected contaminants may inhibit the development of assemblages and may cause measurable but not severe declines in living resources or water quality.
Fair/Poor	Selected contaminants have caused or are likely to cause severe declines in some but not all living resources or water quality.
Poor	Selected contaminants have caused or are likely to cause severe declines in most if not all living resources or water quality.

Habitat
Human Activities

8. | **What are the levels of human activities that may influence habitat quality and how are they changing?**

Human activities that degrade habitat quality do so by affecting structural (geological), biological, oceanographic, acoustic or chemical characteristics. Structural impacts include removal or mechanical alteration, including various fishing techniques (trawls, traps, dredges, longlines and even hook-and-line in some habitats), dredging channels and harbors and dumping spoil, vessel groundings, anchoring, laying pipelines and cables, installing offshore structures, discharging drill cuttings, dragging tow cables, and placing artificial reefs. Removal or alteration of critical biological components of habitats can occur along with several of the above activities, most notably trawling, groundings and cable drags. Marine debris, particularly in large quantities (e.g., lost gill nets and other types of fishing gear), can affect both biological and structural habitat components. Changes in water circulation often occur when channels are dredged, fill is added, coastal areas are reinforced, or other construction takes place. These activities affect habitat by changing food delivery, waste removal, water quality (e.g., salinity, clarity and sedimentation), recruitment patterns and a host of other factors. Acoustic impacts can occur to water column habitats and organisms from acute and chronic sources of anthropogenic noise (e.g., shipping, boating, construction). Chemical alterations most commonly occur following spills and can have both acute and chronic impacts.

Good   Few or no activities occur that are likely to negatively affect habitat quality.

Good/Fair Some potentially harmful activities exist, but they do not appear to have had a negative effect on habitat quality.

Fair   Selected activities have resulted in measurable habitat impacts, but evidence suggests effects are localized, not widespread.

Fair/Poor Selected activities have caused or are likely to cause severe impacts, and cases to date suggest a pervasive problem.

Poor   Selected activities warrant widespread concern and action, as large-scale, persistent and/or repeated severe impacts have occurred or are likely to occur.

Living Resources
Biodiversity

9. | **What is the status of biodiversity and how is it changing?**

This is intended to elicit thought and assessment of the condition of living resources based on expected biodiversity levels and the interactions between species. Intact ecosystems require that all parts not only exist, but that they function together, resulting in natural symbioses, competition and predator-prey relationships. Community integrity, resistance and resilience all depend on these relationships. Abundance, relative abundance, trophic structure, richness, H' diversity, evenness and other measures are often used to assess these attributes.

Good   Biodiversity appears to reflect pristine or near-pristine conditions and promotes ecosystem integrity (full community development and function).

Good/Fair Selected biodiversity loss has taken place, precluding full community development and function, but it is unlikely to cause substantial or persistent degradation of ecosystem integrity.

Fair   Selected biodiversity loss may inhibit full community development and function and may cause measurable but not severe degradation of ecosystem integrity.

Fair/Poor Selected biodiversity loss has caused or is likely to cause severe declines in some but not all ecosystem components and reduce ecosystem integrity.

Poor   Selected biodiversity loss has caused or is likely to cause severe declines in ecosystem integrity.

Living Resources
Extracted
Species

10. | **What is the status of environmentally sustainable fishing and how is it changing?**

Commercial and recreational harvesting are highly selective activities, for which fishers and collectors target a limited number of species, and often remove high proportions of populations. In addition to removing significant amounts of biomass from the ecosystem, reducing its availability to other consumers, these activities tend to disrupt specific and often critical food web links. When too much extraction occurs (i.e. ecologically unsustainable harvesting), trophic cascades ensue, resulting in changes in the abundance of non-targeted species as well. It also reduces the ability of the targeted species to replenish populations at a rate that supports continued ecosystem integrity.

It is essential to understand whether removals are occurring at ecologically sustainable levels. Knowing extraction levels and determining the impacts of removal are both ways that help gain this understanding. Measures for target species of abundance, catch amounts or rates (e.g., catch per unit effort), trophic structure and changes in non-target species abundance are all generally used to assess these conditions.

Other issues related to this question include whether fishers are using gear that is compatible with the habitats being fished and whether that gear minimizes by-catch and incidental take of marine mammals. For example, bottom-tending gear often destroys or alters both benthic structure and non-targeted animal and plant communities. "Ghost fishing" occurs when lost traps continue to capture organisms. Lost or active nets, as well as lines used to mark and tend traps and other fishing gear, can entangle marine mammals. Any of these could be considered indications of environmentally unsustainable fishing techniques.

Good   Extraction does not appear to affect ecosystem integrity (full community development and function).

Good/Fair Extraction takes place, precluding full community development and function, but it is unlikely to cause substantial or persistent degradation of ecosystem integrity.

Fair   Extraction may inhibit full community development and function and may cause measurable but not severe degradation of ecosystem integrity.

Fair/Poor Extraction has caused or is likely to cause severe declines in some but not all ecosystem components and reduce ecosystem integrity.

Poor   Extraction has caused or is likely to cause severe declines in ecosystem integrity.

Living Resources
Non-Indigenous
Species

11. | **What is the status of non-indigenous species and how is it changing?**

Non-indigenous species are generally considered problematic and candidates for rapid response, if found soon after invasion. For those that become established, their impacts can sometimes be assessed by quantifying changes in the affected native species. This question allows sanctuaries to report on the threat posed by non-indigenous species. In some cases, the presence of a species alone constitutes a significant threat (certain invasive algae). In other cases, impacts have been measured and may or may not significantly affect ecosystem integrity.

Good   Non-indigenous species are not suspected or do not appear to affect ecosystem integrity (full community development and function).

Good/Fair Non-indigenous species exist, precluding full community development and function, but are unlikely to cause substantial or persistent degradation of ecosystem integrity.

Fair   Non-indigenous species may inhibit full community development and function and may cause measurable but not severe degradation of ecosystem integrity.

Fair/Poor Non-indigenous species have caused or are likely to cause severe declines in some but not all ecosystem components and reduce ecosystem integrity.

Poor   Non-indigenous species have caused or are likely to cause severe declines in ecosystem integrity.

Living Resources
Key Species

12. | What is the status of key species and how is it changing?

Certain species can be defined as "key" within a marine sanctuary. Some might be keystone species, that is, species on which the persistence of a large number of other species in the ecosystem depends — the pillar of community stability. Their functional contribution to ecosystem function is disproportionate to their numerical abundance or biomass and their impact is therefore important at the community or ecosystem level. Their removal initiates changes in ecosystem structure and sometimes the disappearance of or dramatic increase in the abundance of dependent species. Keystone species may include certain habitat modifiers, predators, herbivores and those involved in critical symbiotic relationships (e.g. cleaning or co-habitating species).

Other key species may include those that are indicators of ecosystem condition or change (e.g., particularly sensitive species), those targeted for special protection efforts, or charismatic species that are identified with certain areas or ecosystems. These may or may not meet the definition of keystone, but do require assessments of status and trends.

Good   Key and keystone species appear to reflect pristine or near-pristine conditions and may promote ecosystem integrity (full community development and function).

Good/Fair Selected key or keystone species are at reduced levels, perhaps precluding full community development and function, but substantial or persistent declines are not expected.

Fair   The reduced abundance of selected keystone species may inhibit full community development and function and may cause measurable but not severe degradation of ecosystem integrity; or selected key species are at reduced levels, but recovery is possible.

Fair/Poor The reduced abundance of selected keystone species has caused or is likely to cause severe declines in some but not all ecosystem components, and reduce ecosystem integrity; or selected key species are at substantially reduced levels, and prospects for recovery are uncertain.

Poor   The reduced abundance of selected keystone species has caused or is likely to cause severe declines in ecosystem integrity; or selected key species are at severely reduced levels, and recovery is unlikely.

Living Resources
Health of Key Species

13. | What is the condition or health of key species and how is it changing?

For those species considered essential to ecosystem integrity, measures of their condition can be important to determining the likelihood that they will persist and continue to provide vital ecosystem functions. Measures of condition may include growth rates, fecundity, recruitment, age-specific survival, tissue contaminant levels, pathologies (disease incidence tumors, deformities), the presence and abundance of critical symbionts, or parasite loads. Similar measures of condition may also be appropriate for other key species (indicator, protected or charismatic species). In contrast to the question about keystone species (#12 above), the impact of changes in the abundance or condition of key species is more likely to be observed at the population or individual level and less likely to result in ecosystem or community effects.

Good   The condition of key resources appears to reflect pristine or near-pristine conditions.

Good/Fair The condition of selected key resources is not optimal, perhaps precluding full ecological function, but substantial or persistent declines are not expected.

Fair   The diminished condition of selected key resources may cause a measurable but not severe reduction in ecological function, but recovery is possible.

Fair/Poor The comparatively poor condition of selected key resources makes prospects for recovery uncertain.

Poor   The poor condition of selected key resources makes recovery unlikely.

Living Resources
Human Activities

14. What are the levels of human activities that may influence living resource quality and how are they changing?

Human activities that degrade living resource quality do so by causing a loss or reduction of one or more species, by disrupting critical life stages, by impairing various physiological processes, or by promoting the introduction of non-indigenous species or pathogens. (Note: Activities that impact habitat and water quality may also affect living resources. These activities are dealt with in Questions 4 and 8, and many are repeated here as they also have direct effect on living resources).

Fishing and collecting are the primary means of removing resources. Bottom trawling, seine-fishing and the collection of ornamental species for the aquarium trade are all common examples, some being more selective than others. Chronic mortality can be caused by marine debris derived from commercial or recreational vessel traffic, lost fishing gear and excess visitation, resulting in the gradual loss of some species.

Critical life stages can be affected in various ways. Mortality to adult stages is often caused by trawling and other fishing techniques, cable drags, dumping spoil or drill cuttings, vessel groundings or persistent anchoring. Contamination of areas by acute or chronic spills, discharges by vessels, or municipal and industrial facilities can make them unsuitable for recruitment; the same activities can make nursery habitats unsuitable. Although coastal armoring and construction can increase the availability of surfaces suitable for the recruitment and growth of hard bottom species, the activity may disrupt recruitment patterns for other species (e.g., intertidal soft bottom animals) and habitat may be lost.

Spills, discharges, and contaminants released from sediments (e.g., by dredging and dumping) can all cause physiological impairment and tissue contamination. Such activities can affect all life stages by reducing fecundity, increasing larval, juvenile, and adult mortality, reducing disease resistance, and increasing susceptibility to predation. Bioaccumulation allows some contaminants to move upward through the food chain, disproportionately affecting certain species.

Activities that promote introductions include bilge discharges and ballast water exchange, commercial shipping and vessel transportation. Releases of aquarium fish can also lead to species introductions.

Good	Few or no activities occur that are likely to negatively affect living resource quality.
Good/Fair	Some potentially harmful activities exist, but they do not appear to have had a negative effect on living resource quality.
Fair	Selected activities have resulted in measurable living resource impacts, but evidence suggests effects are localized, not widespread.
Fair/Poor	Selected activities have caused or are likely to cause severe impacts, and cases to date suggest a pervasive problem.
Poor	Selected activities warrant widespread concern and action, as large-scale, persistent and/or repeated severe impacts have occurred or are likely to occur.

Maritime Archaeological Resources Integrity

15. | What is the integrity of known maritime archaeological resources and how is it changing?

The condition of archaeological resources in a marine sanctuary significantly affects their value for science and education, as well as the resource's eligibility for listing in the National Register of Historic Places. Assessments of archaeological sites include evaluation of the apparent levels of site integrity, which are based on levels of previous human disturbance and the level of natural deterioration. The historical, scientific and educational values of sites are also evaluated and are substantially determined and affected by site condition.

Good — Known archaeological resources appear to reflect little or no unexpected disturbance.

Good/Fair — Selected archaeological resources exhibit indications of disturbance, but there appears to have been little or no reduction in historical, scientific or educational value.

Fair — The diminished condition of selected archaeological resources has reduced, to some extent, their historical, scientific or educational value, and may affect the eligibility of some sites for listing in the National Register of Historic Places.

Fair/Poor — The diminished condition of selected archaeological resources has substantially reduced their historical, scientific or educational value, and is likely to affect their eligibility for listing in the National Register of Historic Places.

Poor — The degraded condition of known archaeological resources in general makes them ineffective in terms of historical, scientific or educational value, and precludes their listing in the National Register of Historic Places.

Maritime Archaeological Resources Threat to Environment

16. | Do known maritime archaeological resources pose an environmental hazard and how is this threat changing?

The sinking of a ship potentially introduces hazardous materials into the marine environment. This danger is true for historic shipwrecks as well. The issue is complicated by the fact that shipwrecks older than 50 years may be considered historical resources and must, by federal mandate, be protected. Many historic shipwrecks, particularly early to mid-20th century, still have the potential to retain oil and fuel in tanks and bunkers. As shipwrecks age and deteriorate, the potential for release of these materials into the environment increases.

Good — Known maritime archaeological resources pose few or no environmental threats.

Good/Fair — Selected maritime archaeological resources may pose isolated or limited environmental threats, but substantial or persistent impacts are not expected.

Fair — Selected maritime archaeological resources may cause measurable, but not severe, impacts to certain sanctuary resources or areas, but recovery is possible.

Fair/Poor — Selected maritime archaeological resources pose substantial threats to certain sanctuary resources or areas, and prospects for recovery are uncertain.

Poor — Selected maritime archaeological resources pose serious threats to sanctuary resources, and recovery is unlikely.

Maritime Archaeological Resources
Human Activities

17. | What are the levels of human activities that may influence maritime archaeological resource quality and how are they changing?

Some human maritime activities threaten the physical integrity of submerged archaeological resources. Archaeological site integrity is compromised when elements are moved, removed or otherwise damaged. Threats come from looting by divers, inadvertent damage by scuba diving visitors, improperly conducted archaeology that does not fully document site disturbance, anchoring, groundings, and commercial and recreational fishing activities, among others.

Good	Few or no activities occur that are likely to negatively affect maritime archaeological resource integrity.
Good/Fair	Some potentially relevant activities exist, but they do not appear to have had a negative effect on maritime archaeological resource integrity.
Fair	Selected activities have resulted in measurable impacts to maritime archaeological resources, but evidence suggests effects are localized, not widespread.
Fair/Poor	Selected activities have caused or are likely to cause severe impacts, and cases to date suggest a pervasive problem.
Poor	Selected activities warrant widespread concern and action, as large-scale, persistent, and/or repeated severe impacts have occurred or are likely to occur.

Notes

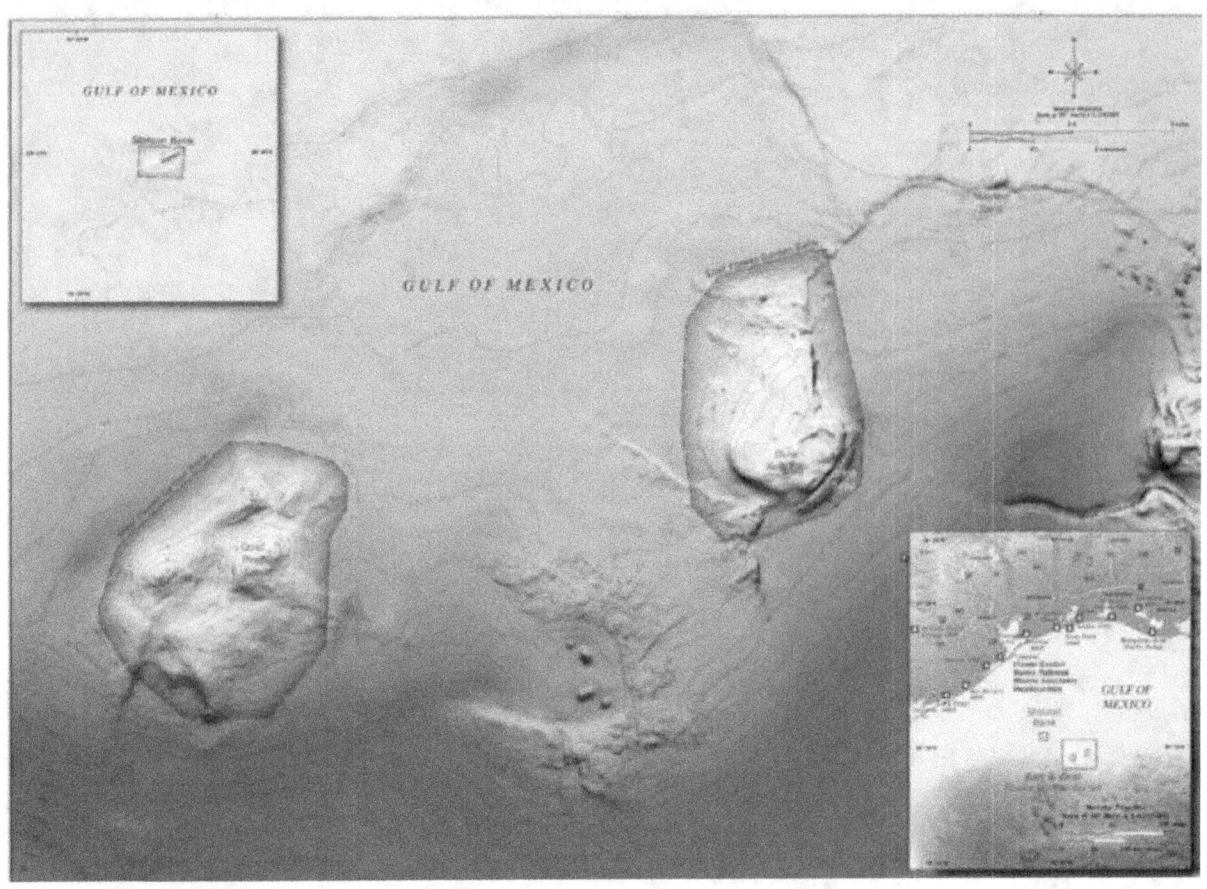

Flower Garden
Banks National Marine Sanctuary